Tommy Bolin

in and out of
Deep Purple

Laura Shenton

sonicbondpublishing.com

Sonicbond Publishing Limited
www.sonicbondpublishing.co.uk
Email: info@sonicbondpublishing.co.uk

First Published in the United Kingdom 2020
First Published in the United States 2020

British Library Cataloguing in Publication Data:
A Catalogue record for this book is available from the British Library

ISBN 978-1-78952-070-5

Typeset in ITC Garamond & ITC Avant Garde
Printed and bound in England

Graphic design and typesetting: Full Moon Media

Tommy Bolin

in and out of Deep Purple

Laura Shenton

sonicbondpublishing.com

This book exists because someone who I look up to told me it was possible. You know who you are. Thank you.

Tommy Bolin
in and out of Deep Purple

Contents

Introduction

Like many people, I became aware of Tommy Bolin through his work with Deep Purple. This book exists because my journey into learning about and enjoying Bolin's music went through a number of stages. Initially, I was of the narrow opinion that I would not enjoy Deep Purple's *Come Taste The Band* album. I used to be in that camp of people who believed 'no Purple without Ritchie Blackmore' and 'Ritchie Blackmore is Deep Purple'. This disproportionately strong bias meant that I didn't bother giving the *Come Taste The Band* album much of my attention.

Until one day I thought to myself, 'People really say some mean things about Tommy Bolin on some of the fan forums. Who is this guy anyway? He must be a pretty big deal if he was considered good enough to meet the standards of a band as awesome as Deep Purple'. It was because of this that I gave Bolin's solo work a listen. The first songs of his that I heard were 'Wild Dogs' from the *Teaser* album and 'Bustin' Out For Rosey' from the *Private Eyes* album. After hearing those two tracks, I was absolutely hooked. I loved the emotion in both Bolin's guitar playing and his vocals, the preciously sentimental lyrics in 'Wild Dogs', and the gorgeous use of the pentatonic scale in 'Bustin' Out For Rosey'. I figured that there really has got to be more to Tommy Bolin than merely being Ritchie Blackmore's replacement in Deep Purple. And that's when something hit me. Even though some very prolific tracks from Bolin's solo career have been on YouTube for a good number of years, some of them have views that don't go beyond five figures and comment sections where the number of posts barely reach into double figures. This made me feel genuinely sad, and I realised that here was a musician of phenomenal talent and yet, not many people seem to know or even care. Like many Bolin fans, I find that incredibly poignant considering that he died so young – at the age of twenty-five.

This book is not embedded in a feeble attempt to elevate the status of one musician above the other. That would be futile. Both Ritchie Blackmore and Tommy Bolin are/were amazing musicians and fascinating people in their own right. It is just that the former seems to have had much more recognition for his work. It is necessary to take a step back and make space to celebrate the contribution that Tommy Bolin made to music in his tragically short life.

In the interest of transparency and providing some context, as the author of this book, I have absolutely no affiliation with Tommy Bolin or his associates. Indeed, I wasn't born until 1988. In writing this book, my aim is to offer an objective narrative regarding the life and music of Tommy Bolin based on my research. This book is an unauthorised project in order to allow the publisher and I full editorial control. Of course, I am very much a fan of Tommy's music (and indeed, Deep Purple) and it matters to me to be able to write about it with fluency and understanding in a way that does justice to Tommy Bolin's legacy. As a result, while Bolin's problem with drugs cannot be denied and it will be mentioned where absolutely relevant, it matters to me not to overshadow the musical aspect of his legacy with the more painful elements of it.

Tommy Bolin's is a story that needs to be told. I refuse to accept that an artist who created such beautiful music can be forgotten in the wisps of time and occasionally footnoted as Blackmore's replacement in Deep Purple. If just one person reads this book and feels that, as a result, they enjoy the *Come Taste The Band* album as a worthwhile piece of work in its own right (don't think of it as post-Blackmore Deep Purple or even as Deep Purple Mk4; that was genuinely the turning point for me) then I will feel that I have done some justice to Tommy Bolin and the beauty of his music.

The narrative of this book does not follow a chronological order. The logic behind this is that it feels important to set the foundations of Tommy Bolin's most public experiences and presence before delving deeper into his music and his life. It is necessary to represent Bolin and his story through the lens of his time in Deep Purple as a means of offering some context. How he was portrayed by the media and how he is often written off by Deep Purple fans needs to be acknowledged due to the way in which it starkly contrasts with the fantastic musician that Bolin was in his creations outside of Deep Purple.

Chapter One: Welcome To The Band

It started off so well. As Jon Lord enthused in October 1975 in *Melody Maker*:

> Tommy can't be so bad for us with so many good ideas. All I can say is when
> you hear the album (*Come Taste The Band*) you'll change your mind.
> Whether you like the music or not, you'll have to realise that Deep Purple now
> have an excitement in their playing that they haven't had in a long time. I've
> always thought that Purple were a band that people saw as 'well yes a big band,
> but I wish they would do more'.

By 1975, Deep Purple had already been through a number of lineups and
musical styles. The Mk1 lineup from 1968 to 1969 featured Jon Lord on keys,
Ian Paice on drums, Ritchie Blackmore on lead guitar, Nick Simper on bass
and Rod Evans on vocals. During this time, Deep Purple were still finding their
feet stylistically and commercially. They were still seen as an underground act
by many and were predominantly marketed towards the hippy culture at the
time on Harvest Records, a division of EMI set up for such market. It was in
1970 that the *Deep Purple In Rock* album epitomised the sound that many have
come to most associate with the band. This masterpiece occurred due to the
second lineup of the band featuring Roger Glover on bass and Ian Gillan on
vocals. They breathed new life into the band having been recruited from their
old band, Episode Six. It was through the second lineup of Deep Purple that
the band became associated with the genre of hard rock and to some extents,
heavy metal. This was the lineup responsible for some of the band's most well-
known songs including 'Smoke On The Water', 'Black Night' and 'Highway
Star'. Stylistically and commercially, this approach to music continued
throughout the Mk3 lineup of Deep Purple which saw Glenn Hughes replacing
Roger Glover on bass and David Coverdale replacing Ian Gillan on vocals in
1973 to create the successful album, *Burn*. Briefly speaking, Deep Purple was
already an established band by the time Tommy Bolin came into the picture.

Despite the frequency of lineup changes, audiences had come to expect
a particular brand of music from Deep Purple. It was heavy, aggressive and
exciting. Further to this, as with Lord and Paice on keys and drums respectively,
Ritchie Blackmore had been the only lead guitarist in the band since it began.
From a personnel perspective, Bolin's recruitment into Deep Purple was
significant because Blackmore had been such a strong driving force in the band
from day one; he was one of the key founders of it (the band was named after his
grandmother's favourite song) and certainly musically and commercially a very
big deal by the time he decided to walk away from Deep Purple in 1975 to form
his band, Rainbow. Coverdale said in August 1975 in the *New Musical Express*:

You gotta remember man, that to replace Ritchie… well, you know. He wasn't just anybody and you can't get just anybody to replace him.

Around the time of the beginning of the Deep Purple Mk4 lineup, there was also a lot of talk from all remaining members of the band that Blackmore's departure was a huge relief because it meant that, particularly regarding live performances, the rest of the band were no longer held to ransom based on the unpredictable nature of what mood Mr Blackmore may have been in that day. It's important to remember that this is a man who once smashed a TV camera to smithereens by jabbing his guitar into it. He threw speakers off the front of the stage and set fire to several large towers of equipment during his infamous California Jam tantrum in 1974. Sure, destroying a guitar or two in the name of art was not untypical of Ritchie Blackmore but as he said himself in several interviews, he was angry that the organisers of the California Jam were pushing for Deep Purple to go on stage before sunset, something he had strongly insisted against from the point of agreeing and indeed signing on the dotted line to do the gig. It wouldn't seem fair to say that Blackmore was/is an angry person. The aggression of his on-stage persona was certainly iconic at times, though! He hated having to mime to studio recordings of Deep Purple's songs to be filmed in television studios; in a comedic act of defiance, there is footage of him miming to 'Fireball' (1971) with his guitar the wrong way round.

Whatever you may think of Blackmore, as a musician or as a character, he was clearly a unique personality to work with. It is understandable as to how his departure from Deep Purple would have inevitably caused a change in dynamics between the remaining members who went on to form Mk4. In his interview with *Melody Maker* in October 1975, Jon Lord continued:

We got stale, tired and old. We became an institution if you like. In fact, we had started to believe our own publicity. They always say that is the prime thing not to do. Ritchie comes in here very strongly. I'm not going to try to make a scapegoat out of him, but the point had been reached where if Ritchie didn't like it, we didn't do it. We all respected him and so we allowed him that freedom, we began to feel if he didn't get his way he would pick up his guitar and go. When he did I was broken-hearted for all of four and a half hours. A flippant remark, but based on fact. The younger element in the band (Coverdale and Hughes) thought f*** it, why do we have to break up just because Ritchie's left and eventually I was caught by their enthusiasm. And that's where Tommy comes in.

By May 1975, Deep Purple were without a guitar player due to Blackmore's departure and were living in Los Angeles due to tax reasons. By June, what was formerly known as Columbia Sound Stage in Hollywood had been rented for auditions and rehearsals. The studio was a large building that had been previously been used by Columbia Pictures for making movies. Sound engineer Robert Simon had taken it over and named it Pirate Sound Studios. Deep Purple had already worked with Simon at their live shows and considered him to be preferable as a sound engineer. He was a natural choice for the band and they were one of the first to work in his new studio. Several guitarists had already been auditioned by Deep Purple. One such guitarist was Dave 'Clem' Clempson who was previously a member of the band, Colosseum. During the time of Clempson's audition, he was still a member of the band, Humble Pie. Clempson's credentials were such that Deep Purple were enthusiastic about auditioning him. However, when it came to the audition itself, Deep Purple felt that he was not a good match for them. Two key reasons for this were that musically he was not what Deep Purple had in mind but also, the chemistry was absent on a personal basis too. In July 1975, David Coverdale explained in *Sounds*:

We got Clem Clempson over from England. He was really good, but he was too much like a Rolling Stones guitarist. We were looking for somebody really incredible. I mean, Jon's played with Blackmore and Albert Lee; and they're two of the greatest guitar players in the world. We have a really high standard to keep up.

Glenn Hughes recalled in his autobiography:

My idea for Blackmore's replacement was Clem Clempson of Humble Pie, a Brummie who was a brilliant guitar player. He came and stayed at my house and we auditioned him and he played great, but he didn't have the charisma that he needed to stand up against Blackmore.

Evidently, it would take somebody very special to pass an audition with Deep Purple. The situation of trying to find a guitarist was becoming desperate and it was getting to the point where Jon Lord was weighing up whether he felt it was worth continuing with the search and indeed Deep Purple, at all. After his death, He was quoted by Geoff Barton in August 2017 in *Classic Rock*:

I was sitting in California thinking: 'This is alright, I've got a few bob in the bank, it's been a good run. I'll just sit here and look at the Pacific and think about what to do next.'

This period of frustration was exemplified when costs of studio time continued to build up with every day that the band was without a guitarist. It was a conversation between Deep Purple roadie, Colin Hart, and Robert Simon that resulted in Tommy Bolin being suggested as a potential candidate. Simon had already been exposed to Tommy's talents as a guitar player when working on the sound for shows that included James Gang, a band in which Tommy had recently played guitar. This suggestion was welcomed by David Coverdale who was both aware and indeed impressed by Tommy's work on Billy Cobham's *Spectrum* album.

During the time of Tommy's audition for Deep Purple, he was already in the early stages of working with Nemperor Records on his first solo album, *Teaser*. As a result of this, Tommy was living nearby in Malibu. Coverdale said in August 1975 in the *New Musical Express*:

> I got on the phone to our agent in New York to find him because I thought he was an East Coaster and he told me Tommy was living just five miles away from me in Malibu. The management were a bit scared when they heard he's played with Cobham: they thought, 'Oh no, a jazz-man'. But I called him up when we were both really stoned and we talked for half an hour about curry and chips and I finally invited him down to a session.

Tommy was accompanied to audition for Deep Purple by his manager at the time, Barry Fey. He was a very high profile influence in the music business by numerous accounts; a bossy but passionate character who was associated with acts such as Ozzy Osbourne, Led Zeppelin, and Jimi Hendrix. As was reported in November 1977 in *Billboard*:

> During the Rolling Stones '72 America tour, Fey handled more shows (sixteen) than any other promoter. In 1976 and again last summer, Feyline's Red Rocks Festival proved itself (to be) one of the industry's most lucrative and prestigious packages, grossing more that one million dollars each year.

The chemistry between Tommy Bolin and the members of Deep Purple was immediate. Equally, there was a shared musical passion and mutual admiration that inspired all parties to want to work with each other. Jon Lord enthused in May 1999 in *Guitar World*:

> I was blown away and utterly entranced by this guitar player. Tommy plugged in and we jammed, and boy was it good!

Bolin was interviewed in November 1975 in *Creem* magazine, where he spoke highly of his experience of auditioning with Deep Purple. The admiration and respect that he had for his new colleagues was evident, as was his enthusiasm for the musical direction his career was moving in around that time as a whole:

> When the Purple first called me for an audition, I hadn't slept in a couple of days, not a wink, 'cause I'd been up writing stuff. The rehearsal was for four o'clock and I was lying there thinking I gotta figure a way to tell 'em, you know, tomorrow or something. And I thought, 'Well, f*** it, I'll just go down'. So I walked in and I was like a zombie. But in the first tune, right away, it was smiles all around. You know, I was shocked to see how good they were, 'cause I had never heard that much Deep Purple.

The honesty with which Bolin spoke of his unfamiliarity with Deep Purple's music is endearing, especially considering how many guitarists would have been keen to join the band purely on the basis that it was Deep Purple. Seemingly, Bolin's acquaintance with Deep Purple was based predominantly on musical chemistry rather than being star-struck. It was in this same interview with *Creem* magazine that Bolin admitted to only having heard 'Smoke On The Water' when he was asked to audition with Deep Purple. Bolin's shared passion for making music with Deep Purple is something that he further commented on in the *Creem* magazine interview:

> I've done all-night sessions with Jon, Ian, Glenn, you know, with each of them individually, and they're amazing players. Why they haven't stuck out, why Ritchie has stuck out more than the rest of 'em, I don't know… I don't want to hide behind my amps or nothing, but I want to see an end to the image of guitar player out front and the band in back. We're doing a lot of my tunes and, with the stuff I'm writing, I'm trying to bring in the talent of the whole group. And in the live show – we're planning to tour early next year – everybody'll be featured.

It is striking from Bolin's comments in his interview with *Creem* magazine that he was excited to join Deep Purple and that they were pleased to have him in the band. The beginning of Deep Purple Mk4 looked set to be a beautiful collaboration of five musicians who got on with each other and were musically on the same page. The dream team for the Mk4 Deep Purple had now been established as Jon Lord on keys, Ian Paice on drums, Glenn Hughes on bass (with additional vocals), David Coverdale on vocals and of course, Tommy Bolin on guitar. Bolin's comments about wanting to utilise all of the band's talents seem to portray him as a good team player. Surely this could only be a good thing for a band that had recently gone through such a turbulent and dramatic change of lineups over the years. Although lineup changes were not unfamiliar territory to Deep Purple, it was considered by many that Blackmore's departure from the band was a big deal. Blackmore had a reputation as the moody man in black, largely responsible for both the aggressive stage persona of the band, as well as musically, the distinctive riffs that elevated them to such prominence. Equally though, Bolin spoke to *Creem* magazine with honesty about his solo projects that he had committed to before joining Deep Purple:

> I consider myself a full member of the group, but Deep Purple isn't gonna take up that much of my time each year. The other months, I'll probably go out with my own band, which'll probably include different players each time. (Deep Purple are) happy that I'm gonna play solo and that I'm doing my own album because what's good for me is good for them and vice versa. I'm glad that it's started off this way. It seems when you're in a band for a while and you say, 'O.K., I wanna do my own album', it's like the other people are thinking, 'Well, maybe he doesn't dig what's happening here'. But since I started my own album before I met them, it's a different attitude. Also, they know I would've loved to have them on my record. I tried like hell to get 'em to come play on it, but they can't record in the States. Taxes or something, something weird. So that's why they're recording in Munich... and why I'll probably do my next one there because I want them on it. They're just phenomenal players.

In June 1975, *Melody Maker* featured an interview with Bolin discussing his new venture with Deep Purple. The interview was appropriately titled, 'Bolin: A New Light' and this seems very much reflective of the mood at the time as in, Deep Purple, the media and indeed Bolin himself spoke optimistically of the breath of fresh air that would be Mk4 Deep Purple. Bolin surmised in the interview:

> I want the band (Deep Purple) to sound as powerful as the old Purple, but fresh. We've been jamming a lot, on all kinds of tunes, even 'Lullaby Of Birdland' (a jazz standard written by George Shearing and George David Weiss in 1952) just to familiarise ourselves with each other.

It is exciting to think that there was so much potential for creativity in the new lineup of Deep Purple. That's not to say that there was an absence of it in the lineups before Mk4 because that would not even be slightly true as in, all Deep Purple albums are worth listening to and have all been successful (even if such success occurred years later such as with the 1968 album, *The Book of Taliesyn*). However, the introduction of Bolin to Deep Purple was very much promoted as a positive influence that would inject new enthusiasm into the band that some felt was lacking in the buildup to Blackmore eventually calling it a day and going on to form Rainbow in 1975. In July 1975, Jon Lord advocated in *Sounds:*

> To replace someone like Ritchie in a band is a gamble and that's why I'm excited because I think Purple will either go up or down. I don't think it will carry on as it's been and that's what's exciting. It could either become bigger or we could just disappear and die. For the first time in a long while, we've got something to fight for.

Of course, Deep Purple Mk2 did reunite in 1984 for the tour and similarly named album, *Perfect Strangers*, but the fact remains that in 1975 nobody had a crystal ball and it was generally considered at the time that Ritchie Blackmore had left Deep Purple for good. Equally, by the time Deep Purple had split in 1976, it was considered that this was a final decision. This was reported in July 1976 in the *New Musical Express*:

> After months of speculation about their future, Deep Purple officially announced this week that they have broken up. Rumours of a possible split have been widespread for some time and, until recently, have always been met with denials. But now an official statement, issued on behalf of the band, says that they 'will not record or perform together as Deep Purple again'. The final decision was taken last week by the current members, together with their manager Rob Cooksey. It is described as a culmination of a series of personnel changes over the last few years, the last being the departure of Ritchie Blackmore just over a year ago.

Similarly, in July 1976 in *Record Mirror*, this was reported about the band's split:

> Deep Purple's own record label, Purple, will remain 'dormant'.

Possibly as a result of the shared sense of finality in the band's mileage in 1976, several candid interviews took place with regards to some of the band's darker experiences. The tour of Jakarta will feature in the next chapter. It is a painful and unpleasant tale, but it is certainly not something that can be overlooked.

Chapter Two: Touring Pains

Tommy had not long joined Deep Purple before it was time for the band to tour. Touring had started well. The first stop was Honolulu, Hawaii on the 8 November 1975. *Billboard* reviewed the concert in a favourable light in December 1975:

> Deep Purple won over their audience in Hawaii with a fusion of their hard rock standards and new material from their just-released LP. Bolin made few mistakes in his debut and succeeded in not only filling Blackmore's shoes but also pumping new vitality into a band that after eight years and ten albums, was getting rather stale.

Deep Purple Mk4 were playing well in New Zealand and Australia too. Jon Lord mused in *Record World* in June 1976:

> I think the tour of Australia is one of the happiest tours I've ever been on, that part of it was an incredibly happy time.

Hughes recalled in his autobiography:

> In November 1975, we started our first tour with Tommy, the Australia/Asia tour, which started off in Honolulu in Hawaii. That was a successful first show, and we went on to New Zealand and then had a great run through Australia. We were galvanised as a band by Tommy... The shows were great, all through New Zealand and Australia – The Melbourne shows were great, people still talk about them today... It was six weeks of nirvana and it was a great time. The crew were great, the guys were getting on great. It was the calm before the storm.

Tommy was welcomed with enthusiasm not only by the band but by fans who were supportive of *Teaser*. If the rest of the tour had continued with the same positivity that was apparent at the beginning of it, this could be a different story entirely. Bolin reminisced in *The Drummer* in January 1976:

> One night in Australia, we even did 'Waltzing Matilda' in the middle of one number. Incredible response too.

The next stage of the tour was Jakarta and it was nothing short of disastrous. For Bolin, this was quite the baptism of fire. And they say that Roger Glover and Ian Gillan had a baptism of fire when, not long after having joined Deep

Purple Mk2, they had to play with an orchestra in the *Concerto For Group And Orchestra* performance initiated by Jon Lord in 1969!

On the 4 and 5 December, Deep Purple played at Senayan Sports Stadium in Jakarta, Indonesia. After playing the first show, the band returned to the hotel where the roadie Patsy Collins (who was also Tommy's bodyguard) fell to his death in an elevator shaft. A police investigation revealed it to be an accident, but at the time, Rob Cooksey (the band's manager) and Glenn Hughes were arrested due to the incident. They were released in time for the second show on 5th December, where they were escorted onto the stage at gunpoint. The show was stopped halfway through when the audience were violently attacked by police and guard dogs. This was because the audience was standing and dancing, something that was discouraged in the dictatorship of Jakarta at the time. In Chris Charlesworth's 1983 book, *Deep Purple: The Illustrated Biography*, the band were candid in interviews, describing how they saw members of the audience, including young children, attacked by dogs to the point of bleeding and ripped limbs. The band had to make a run for it to their plane and even then the authorities were trying to make it very difficult for them to leave regarding technical problems with the plane. They were harassed all the way. It is a relief to think that they all managed to escape the violence. Clearly traumatic by any stretch of the imagination, such events must have been incredibly detrimental for morale as the tour continued. Such was the dreadfulness of Jakarta that Bolin's guitar technician, Dave Brown, decided to resign with immediate effect. Brown explained in October 1989 in *Westword*:

> When I left, it was because things were crazy, and I couldn't handle it. The person I saw (Tommy) scared me to death. This guy was tired of his own company.

The next stop was Japan on 8 December 1975. It is rumoured that Tommy's usual choice of drug consumption consisted of snorting heroin due to a fear of needles. In Japan, however, possibly marred by the horrifying experiences from Jakarta, Tommy supposedly injected heroin in a way that caused some temporary damage to his arm. The numbness that ensued was such that it was feared it would compromise the quality of his playing. This was very bad timing for Tommy and the band because Deep Purple's Japanese record company was set on making a live album there. There is a contrasting rumour that Tommy's arm injury was just as a result of having passed out and slept on it for a solid eight hours. Another rumour exists, as was reported in March 1976 in *Circus*, that Tommy's arm injury was derived from an acupuncture session that went wrong. Either way, this was the band's first chance to show what they were capable of in a live setting to a wider audience and by many, Tommy was considered to have compromised it. The recording wasn't released until 1977 – so posthumously for Tommy and after Deep Purple had split. *Last Concert In Japan* features an edited version of Deep Purple playing at the Japan Budokan on 15 December 1975.

The American leg of the tour started in January 1976. It is plausible that Tommy had a better time of it in America because he already had a supportive fan base there due to being known for his music before Deep Purple. He was on familiar territory and bands he had been in previously such as Zephyr and James Gang already had a following there. In September 2003 in *Classic Rock*, journalist Geoff Barton considered that Tommy played fantastically in Texas in the February of 1976. He also candidly referred to witnessing first hand the enormity of the drugs problem shared by both Tommy and Glenn Hughes at the time.

Throughout their time in Deep Purple, Tommy and Glenn shared a friendship based not only on their musical interests but on their shared drug problem. It created much tension within the band. Jon Lord and Ian Paice were more experienced with the rock and roll lifestyle and were much calmer about it by this point in their careers whereas Tommy and Glenn were going wild. This left a confused and alienated David Coverdale stuck in the middle of it all. The quality of experiences of the live shows seemed to differ both for the band as well as the audience. Sometimes the band played well to a supportive fan base. On other occasions, musical differences, egos, and drug-related issues put a dampener on things. Equally, the whole 'Bolin isn't Blackmore' issue wouldn't seem to leave. This was particularly the case when the band played the British leg of the tour. Coverdale complained in March 1976 in *Melody Maker*:

I still think we're asking too much of our audience. We start giving no-nonsense rock, with no subtleties. Then we go on to the solo spots and everybody does their own things. It's really unnecessary to overindulge to the point that we do. I think that we should just go on and play to the people. I'd rather be regarded as an entertainer than a prima donna. The messing about can be done in the studio… I don't see Purple as a group, you see. It's a concept. The musical interests in the band are so diverse and so stretched out that the idea of rock can sometimes get lost. Sometimes people put in their alternative interests and that can take away the essence. It's frustrating as f*** to be honest. Being part of a concept can be very limiting if you're not an instrumentalist. I'd rather run round the stage than be sitting in the dressing room having a smoke when somebody's doing the solo bit. You've also got to remember that Purple is five instrumentalists, five egomaniacs, fighting for the limelight.

When playing in Leicester there were calls for Blackmore. Coverdale commented to *Melody Maker*:

> If Tommy wants to blow it, he can blow it. He got a bit uptight at Leicester. He was doing a solo piece and it could only take one guy or chick to shout 'Blackmore' to throw it. For two years I was answering questions about Ian Gillan. It's something you have to live with and get over. The thing about Tommy is that he's been replacing people all the time. He replaced Joe Walsh in the James Gang and then Ritchie in Purple. I suppose he's got a bit of a chip on his shoulder. It's all a matter really of maturity and believing in yourself. Tommy is a gypsy nomad in guitar land. He can either show breathtaking genius or be very mundane. Usually, he's breathtaking.

There is so much to say about Coverdale's comments to *Melody Maker*. Not being a fan of each other soloing is something that many bands often complain about. It could be an ego thing, and it has an almost *Spinal Tap* feel to it. Musically, there is a need to create something for the audience rather than something that is based on self-indulgence. There is such a fine line between an excellent solo and someone playing for the sake of being heard. So of course, Coverdale's comments about the soloing could be considered somewhat redundant on the basis that it is drastically subject to musical taste and opinion. However, his remark about Ian Gillan is of interest in terms of how it references how Coverdale coped with being Gillan's replacement when Deep Purple transitioned from their second to their third lineup.

For Tommy Bolin, he had to fill the shoes of Ritchie Blackmore who had been a member of Deep Purple since being a founder of the band. Arguably there is a considerable difference of experience when comparing Bolin's of joining Deep Purple to Coverdale's. When you look at the timeline of the band, Bolin's presence feels chronologically like a footnote compared to Blackmore's, especially when taking into account the band's history as a whole. When Mk2 Deep Purple reformed in 1984, Blackmore was active on four studio albums, having played on nine studio albums before Bolin's one album with the band. It becomes apparent how it is all too easy for Bolin's contribution to Deep Purple to be too readily overlooked. Even around the time of the Mk2 reunion, examples exist of where the media were derogatory to Tommy Bolin's legacy as a member of Deep Purple. In July 1984 in *Radio & Records*, it was stated:

> The late Tommy Bolin as Blackmore's understudy managed to record only one album, *Come Taste The Band*, before Deep Purple finally split up for the time being.

Understudy? Really? Come on *Radio & Records*, have at least some class! It is this sort of slating that warrants this book. Tommy Bolin was so much more than Ritchie Blackmore's understudy.

The calls from the audience for Blackmore seem so misplaced when you take into account how musically different Tommy was. Blackmore and Bolin were worlds apart. Firstly, Blackmore's musical background was based on his classical training in the guitar from a young age – his father told him that if he did not get good at the guitar and take it seriously, he would hit him round the head with it. Although Blackmore seems to have spoken of this humorously in interviews, there is certainly a poignancy to it as, alongside this, he often talks about how such an upbringing informed many personal struggles in the lexicon of striving for perfection and not feeling good enough. Blackmore's classical training in guitar, combined with his love of music by Bach, informed much of his musical inspiration. For instance, Blackmore's solos on both 'Highway Star' and 'Burn' are based on Bach inspired chord progressions, with melodic patterns and intervals that are reflective of that. In 1975 when Blackmore was promoting Rainbow's first album, *Ritchie Blackmore's Rainbow*, there were many interviews in which he spoke of the enthusiasm he had for being able to expand upon his interest in using classical music influences. He said that while in Deep Purple, he was already making music that had a strong classical influence but that he was excited to be able to do this more in Rainbow because creatively and commercially, he had more control over his new band. In particular, the *Ritchie Blackmore's Rainbow* album uses a number of features that are inspired by medieval music and this is very much apparent on the track 'Sixteenth Century Greensleeves'. Add to this the fact that Blackmore was renowned for creating music that was very riff orientated and again, this all stands in strong contrast to where Tommy Bolin was coming from as a musician.

Bolin was predominantly a self-taught guitarist. He asserted in October 1976 in *Circus:*

I started off on Hawaiian Steel. I didn't want to, but for some reason, the guy said to start on Hawaiian steel. Mr Flood was his name. He tuned the guitar to the E-ninth, which is the real Hawaiian, but I would never play it – I'd always stand in front of the mirror at home and put on the records and pretend I was playing rock. Mr Flood didn't know Elvis. He liked Hawaiian music. So I left that and started taking lessons from this lady, Mrs Sullivan, who had an unbelievable collection of guitars. She had tons of them. And she was very country and western. I started off reading, and the first song I learned how to read was 'On Top Of Ol' Smokey', but I thought, this isn't it either. So then I went to another place, the music store where all the bands hung out, all my local heroes, but what they taught me wasn't it either. Finally what happened was I started playing along on Rolling Stones records.

On balance, Blackmore was not a rigidly trained classical musician; he has stipulated in multiple interviews that he doesn't sight read and prefers to use chord sheets teamed with his knowledge of music theory. However, Bolin's training background certainly comes across as more casual than Blackmore's. This is absolutely no criticism of either artist or either method of training. Again, to try to elevate one above the other seems inappropriate because they are clearly both excellent musicians, albeit different. Bolin's influences were based more in jazz, Latin and blues. This is apparent on the *Come Taste The Band* album where Bolin has writing credits on seven of the album's nine songs. *Come Taste The Band* is stylistically different to the albums that Deep Purple made when Blackmore was there. For example, the funk influence on *Come Taste The Band* is so prominent that the bridge section of the song, 'Gettin' Tighter' would not sound out of place on an Ian Dury And The Blockheads song! Glenn Hughes said of 'Gettin' Tighter' in his autobiography:

> Tommy and I wrote this at my house in Beverly Hills, late one night. What you see is what you get with this one.

When considering the distinctive musical differences between Blackmore and Bolin, it becomes understandable that it was inevitable that Bolin would be bringing a very different style of writing, playing and general creativity to Deep Purple. To really appreciate, and indeed enjoy, Bolin's contribution to Deep Purple, it seems almost illogical to compare him to Blackmore. Musically, they were like chalk and cheese. To expect Bolin to continue where Blackmore left off may have been unrealistic. But then, the question perhaps lies in asking whether Deep Purple recruited Bolin with the aim of having someone to follow in Blackmore's footsteps or were they excited about the new musical approach that Bolin would bring to the band? Was he there because he was a good guitarist and there were financial obligations to continue the band? A multitude of factors informed the decision because Deep Purple were renowned for being a band of many conflicting egos. Either way, it is plausible that Bolin was unlucky when it came to working with Deep Purple. It was an opportunity to play with a big name band but considering that many fans were hung up on the 'he's not Blackmore' issue and Deep Purple were considering calling it a day even before even meeting Bolin, it's understandable that his time with the band could have been quite painful.

There is a sense that Bolin perhaps felt considerably alienated from Deep Purple and indeed the band's fans at times. He said in *Sounds* in July 1976:

People would come up and say 'Hey is it true you hold the *Guinness Book Of Records* as being the world's loudest band?' and I'd say 'I don't know, I wasn't even in the band at the time'.

Deep Purple's concert at Long Beach Arena was reviewed positively in *Record World* in March 1976. It included praise for Tommy and his contribution to the band. This was one of the later shows in a tour that is predominantly looked back on as the band being in turmoil by this point. It just goes to show that there were good days even when things seemed to be going wrong overall. The overriding narrative of the *Come Taste The Band* tour is a story of things going from bad to worse but of course, it is necessary to consider that there would have been people who still enjoyed Bolin's work with Deep Purple; not all of the later concerts of the tour could have been absolutely bad for all concerned. The review advocated:

> Bolin is perhaps not the show-stealing technoflash (sic) guitarist that Ritchie Blackmore was, but he is a confident, capable and often exciting guitarist who is every bit as stage-worthy as his predecessor. The test of Bolin's mettle was how strongly the new compositions from *Come Taste The Band* would hold up in comparison with the old standbys like 'Smoke On The Water' or 'Highway Star'. Surprisingly enough, on the new tunes – especially 'Lady Luck' and the current single, 'Gettin' Tighter' – the band sounded more like a unit than at any time in recent memory. Much of this might be attributed to Bolin, who is not intimidated by the need to share the airspace with his cohorts, Hughes, Coverdale, Lord and Paice.

With the American stretch of the tour concluding in Denver on 4 March 1976, Deep Purple travelled to the UK and only succeeded to commit to five shows, after which the band broke up with immediate effect to the extent that the pending part of the tour in Germany was cancelled. Mk4 were predominantly not well received by UK concert goers. It is understandable that the band didn't play many shows there. In July 1976, *New Musical Express* reported:

> After a long spell out of the country, the band arrived here earlier this year to say 'thank you' to their loyal fans. Their Wembley gigs proved to be embarrassingly poor, and rumours of the band's demise grew stronger.

The 'he's not Blackmore' issue plausibly had a profound influence on Tommy's morale and in turn, this had a negative effect on the entire band. In March 1976 in *Melody Maker*, Chris Welch reviewed Deep Purple's gig that took place on Friday 12 March 1976 at London's Empire Pool, Wembley:

This review should have been written in the white heat of anger after seeing Deep Purple play at the Empire Pool, Wembley, on Friday night. But now, several hours have elapsed, it's Monday morning and it doesn't seem to matter anymore. We learn the various reasons for the sad and dismal performance by the band: that they were suffering from jet lag, that Tommy Bolin was reputedly carried on stage to play, that the following night they redeemed themselves. But the fact remains that the whole atmosphere surrounding the Pool was so depressing that it aroused me in feelings of pity for the audience, pity for the musicians and pity for the stewards, who not only had to endure the caterwauling din that Purple produced in the name of rock music, but attempt to control and pacify the anguish and torment the music seemed to induce in the young fans. Quite apart from the spectacle of once-respected musicians degrading themselves, the spectacle of unhappy youth seeking some escape from the seeming vacuity of their lives was worrying and depressing.

The Empire Pool, an echoing, concrete, bear-baiting pit, is eminently unsuitable for musical events. But this was hardly a musical event: just a band out to prove its position on the prestige scale and on occasion to sell hot dogs and tee-shirts and all the tatty paraphernalia of the cheap circus this end of rock has become. That some of the audience enjoyed themselves was undeniable. There were cheers, but there were also perceptive yells of 'rubbish' during Tommy Bolin's main guitar feature. His playing was deeply disappointing, combining all the worst excesses of the fraudulent lead guitarist satirised by rock's own sternest critics, Alberto Y Lost Trios Paranoias. But there was no need for satire with this kind of cheap gimmickry. Unaccompanied, Bolin paused for minutes on end to egg the baying mob to further yelling, then savaged his guitar strings in a parody of the great, flamboyant guitarists who once vitalised rock.

I was sorry to see the great musician and gentleman, Jon Lord, involved in this mess, and his playing when audible though the PA, revealed flashes of his old love for jazz. The only man who emerged with credit was Ian Paice, whose immaculate, ever-enthusiastic drumming, even in the most uncompromising circumstances, held the band together. David Coverdale's screaming vocals were delivered with some heat, but didn't he yearn to sing something of quality and real soul and not all these cheap wine and downers anthems for a zombie? Around the hall, while the band were winning their final encore by sheer brute force, I watched attendants struggle to retain a demented youth, while another lay slumped on the concrete floor. Music should not dispense despair, it should bring hope and joy. There is enough stress in society generated by God knows how many forces, without rock music feeding the process, and peddling aural narcotics.

It is likely that Chris Welch had low expectations for the gig before even attending it. The doubts surrounding Bolin's abilities as a live performer were already public knowledge by then. It could be the case that he described things in a dramatically harsh way for several reasons, either poetic or personal opinion. In the interest of being objective, it *could* have been a good performance in the opinion of a different reviewer. It *could* be the case that the concert was brilliant and that Welch had already decided to give it a bad review before the first note was even played. However, the review is sadly plausible on the basis that it was of a gig that took place just days before Deep Purple decided to declare Liverpool's Empire Theatre their final gig of the tour.

It was after the show, on 15 March 1976 at Liverpool's Empire Theatre, that Jon Lord, Ian Paice and David Coverdale decided that they would quit Deep Purple with immediate effect. Glenn Hughes made an apology to the audience during this show because he felt that the band was underperforming. Jon and Ian were offended by this because it was felt that it wasn't up to Hughes to apologise on anyone else's behalf. As with any band breakup, a myriad of reasons were presented to the media and as ever, conflicting accounts by a range of individuals inevitably fails to provide a definitive answer for the split. However, it does seem undeniable that as a band, Deep Purple Mk4 had reached a point where the ship had become impossible to steer. To put it metaphorically, too many waves, too much turbulence, too many potential directions and nobody agreeing on which one to take.

As much as Tommy and Glenn were good friends, tensions between the two were apparently present when *Come Taste The Band* and *Teaser* were being promoted in America at the same time. After all the dramas on the Deep Purple tour, Tommy was to face more heartache when his long-term girlfriend, Karen Ulibarri, left him for Glenn Hughes. Hughes recalled in his autobiography:

On the day of the Hawaii gig, I wasn't at soundcheck for some reason and Tommy's girlfriend Karen Ulibarri came up to my room. We couldn't keep our hands off each other. It was one of those moments in life where you just don't think. I wasn't thinking 'I want to go and shag my guitar player's girlfriend', I really liked her. She liked me as well. And I don't think she and Tommy were exclusive, he also had a girlfriend that he was seeing in LA. She was extremely seductive, and I have to be honest with you, you could not not want to make love to her.

Hughes and Ulibarri got married and remained as such until their divorce in the autumn of 1988. Hughes stipulated that in the long run, Bolin was accepting of the decision that Karen Ulibarri had made:

> He knew I was with Karen and he was totally fine with that. He told me to go take care of Karen, knowing that we were fond of each other. Tommy gave me the green light – not in a sexual way, but as a brother – to take care of her, never knowing that in the end, I would be taking care of her after his death.

Still, this all seems painful considering that Tommy's enthusiasm for joining Deep Purple seemed to reward him poorly. With the exception of raising his publicity as a musician, by the time he had left the band he had an intense heroin addiction. That's not to say that the situation was one of cause and effect because clearly, addiction and personal decisions are always going to be complex and varied no matter what is going on in someone's life. However, it is unrealistic to say that by the time Tommy had finished with Deep Purple, he had not come away from the experience unscathed. Bolin came to such prominence in the public eye via a route with Deep Purple that was inevitably emotionally challenging. There were times where it was messy and unkind. It seems that Deep Purple treated Tommy in a way that was alienating, particularly in their failure to communicate with him. In an interview with *Sounds* in July 1976, Tommy said:

> I still don't think I am officially out of Purple. I just said 'Look I'll be available at the end of the month, but right now, since you haven't written me, since you haven't done anything…' The only person who came to see me (when Bolin debuted his own band at the Roxy in Los Angeles) was Ian Paice, and we were probably the most distant... I still don't really know where I stand. Since I left the tour they haven't called me, they haven't written me a letter, and somehow I feel like in a way maybe the management was using me, you know because if you care about a person you do those things. I mean, what's it cost to send a telegram? Nothing compared to the money they have, and they didn't even do that. And they knew. They knew what was going on.

On balance, though, the fact that Deep Purple was no more came as news to Glenn Hughes too. Hughes quoted David Coverdale in his autobiography:

> I remember flying over for Ian Paice's wedding, and Glenn came running up to me saying he'd seen the error of his ways, or whatever, and he couldn't wait to start working together again. He had no idea I'd left Purple. Nobody had bothered to tell him. I think it was very difficult for him at that time to realise the Purple party was over.

In an interview with *Modern Drummer* in 1984, Ian Paice said:

> As good a player as he (Bolin) was in the studio, he was hopeless on stage. When he got on a big stage, he just seemed to freeze up. Instead of playing a solo, he'd end up shouting at the audience and arguing with them. Plus there were his personal problems, which didn't help at all. That's when it became too much.

Inevitably though, it seems that Bolin had to deal with a lot on stage, both with Deep Purple and James Gang. In December 1975 in *Circus Raves*, Bolin discussed some of the frustrations of having to deal with hecklers:

> If someone yells 'Where's Blackmore?' at one of our concerts I'll just do what I did when people yelled 'Where's Joe Walsh?' at me while I was with the James Gang. I'll have cards printed up with his address and throw them out to the audience.

Evidently, Bolin was prepared for being heckled as Blackmore's replacement in Deep Purple; he had experienced the same in James Gang for similar reasons. Being seen as the stand-in for someone else is tough and it is a shame that Bolin had to deal with this rather than simply go on stage and play music, the thing that he was truly talented at. To expect heckling can't be a positive experience for any musician; understandably it compromises the quality of the performance. In November 2016 in *Classic Rock* Glenn Hughes said:

> The shouts for Blackmore were overwhelming. And Tommy just could not deal with that. A young man growing musically, mentally, or spiritually couldn't deal with that aspect. He basically gave everybody the finger, and he played below par.

In June 1976, Hughes told *Record World*:

> (Tommy is) affected by things that happen during the day. If he's got to go on at night time and he's had a bad day or something, he'll feel it. Tommy Bolin to me is the best guitar player in the world. Then again he has his ups and downs, but the thing you've got to admire about Tommy is that he's a very sensitive person and if he's not feeling too good then obviously he won't play his best.

There are many live performances of Tommy's that have been released posthumously (see discography). The quality of his playing, both technically and soulfully, speak for themselves. Be sure to listen to Bolin (or indeed any musician) at their best and then make up your own mind. In November 1984 in *Sounds*, Jon Lord said:

> And poor old Tommy, God rest his soul, was out of his depth in this kind of music, he didn't understand what Purple audiences wanted and needed, and we ended up with an album that was absolutely nothing to do with Deep Purple.

This is a disappointing comment to read when taking into account how excited and enthusiastic Jon Lord was about working with Tommy after auditioning him. It also seems ironic that the musical styles of Tommy Bolin that first endeared Deep Purple to him became one of the very things that Bolin was criticised for when it all went wrong. In fairness to Jon Lord, in much later interviews, he spoke highly of the *Come Taste The Band* album and considered that it was good in its own right, it was just misplaced to call it a Deep Purple album. Another thing to consider is that when Bolin joined Deep Purple he had a wealth of experience in playing both hard rock (with James Gang and Moxy) and jazz fusion (with Billy Cobham and Alphonse Mouzon). However, this was hardly exceptional, as all the members of Deep Purple held a range of different musical interests, something that made the band so exciting and capable. Jon Lord, for instance, was classically trained in piano and had passed exams with the Royal College of Music. He was the driving force behind the Deep Purple Mk2 *Concerto For Group And Orchestra* and his solo works included albums that were strongly based on classical music (for example, *Sarabande* in 1976 and *Before I Forget* in 1982. Give them a listen, they are brilliant). So surely, to fault Bolin for being his own person in terms of his musical influences and interests would be pointless; everyone who has ever been in Deep Purple has been celebrated for (both in their individual careers and with the band itself) their ability to make damn good music across a range of genres and styles.

Once off the Deep Purple rollercoaster, Tommy quickly returned to California and began work for his album, *Private Eyes*, as well as touring with the Tommy Bolin Band.

Chapter Three: Humble and Nomadic Beginnings

As a person and musician, Tommy Bolin's background was drastically humble in comparison to the dizzying highs of life with Deep Purple. Being thrust into a heavily critical public eye and working with a band that was marred by much baggage in the form of strong egos and conflicting ideas, could easily have been demoralising. There is no way of telling if life with Deep Purple may or may not have been a factor in Bolin developing the drug habit that would ultimately lead to his demise. Such is the complexity of any kind of addiction that comes with such devastating effects. Either way though, it is imperative to consider Bolin's background in honour of his memory; there was certainly more to him than his drug habit and his turbulent days in Deep Purple.

Thomas Richard Bolin was born on 1 August 1951 in Sioux City, Iowa, to Barbara Jean Bolin (24 January 1924 – 2 February 1994) and Richard Stanley Bolin (25 February 1919 – 12 September 1992). Tommy had two brothers; Richard E. Bolin (24 January 1957 – 24 August 1994) and a younger brother, Johnnie Bolin. Johnnie played drums in Tommy's band during the tour for the *Private Eyes* album. Johnnie is still active as a musician today and has been involved with organising a number of events and releases in relation to Tommy's legacy.

Numerous sources suggest that throughout his life and his music, Tommy's parents were laid back and supportive of him. They were happy to buy him a guitar when he developed a fixation with Elvis at an early age after seeing him perform live in concert. At just five years old, Tommy considered this a defining moment; this was the moment he realised his passion when he knew that he wanted to be a musician of some kind. Bolin's parents had a very relaxed attitude to his disinterest in school, although he was hard working when it came to music. He played covers in two local neighbourhood bands, Denny And The Triumphs and Patch Of Blue respectively. Indeed, such was the support from Tommy's parents that his father would sometimes drive Patch Of Blue to and from gigs, even if it meant staying up all night when he had to get ready for work just a few hours later. Music education wasn't really available at Tommy's school. As Bolin relayed to *Circus* in October 1976:

> It (school) was a waste. I was getting into guitar and wanted to take a music theory course. Well, I found out that they only offered it in alternate years. Where's that at? Do they teach English every other year?

His disillusion with formal education continued and at fifteen, the school insisted that he leave due to the length of his hair. Speaking in *Circus* in October 1976, Tommy said:

> I got kicked out of school when I was fifteen, just approaching sixteen, for my hair. I said, 'Who's complaining, which teacher?' and he (the headteacher) goes, 'The teachers aren't complaining, the kids are'. I said, 'Okay, here's what I'll do: Before each class I'll stand up in front of the room, and if one person objects, I'll cut my hair'. But he said they didn't do it that way. I remember the seniors cutting everybody's hair but mine because I would always hang out with the seniors. The leader of the pack was a guy named Stan. Stan and Dan. Twins. One was a hardcore 'can't-wait-to-get-into-the-army' guy. That was Dan. Stan was like a freak, a real freak, and a really good bass player.

It seems that Tommy was unafraid to be himself, to question the norms imposed on him and to stand up to authority from a young age. Bolin's mother, Barbara, fully supported her son's decision to question the school's rules and did not pressure him to return there. Her philosophy was that if the school could not accept him as he was then why should he be obliged to accept them. His parents' relaxed attitude was such that Tommy didn't feel it necessary to go back to school and at the age of sixteen they supported him in his decision to leave the family home. Bolin's brother Johnnie, speaking in November 2016 in *Classic Rock* said:

> Mom and dad were behind him one hundred per cent. I mean, to let a kid go hitchhike to Denver, it's not like they didn't care, but he said: 'That's what I really want to do'. And my mom didn't like the fact that they kept throwing him out of school because of his long hair.

In the October 1976 *Circus* magazine interview, Tommy spoke about the laid back and open-minded attitude that surrounded him as he grew up:

> When you come from the Midwest, you have a more open mind than if you come from the West Coast or the East Coast. At that time you had vagrants, rich kids and everything. My family were all musicians. I had a leather jacket and combed my hair back. As I said, I've always been surrounded by music. That's all I wanted to do. I really wasn't interested in school or anything. When I first coloured my hair, my mother loved it. She wanted to do it, but I said no. She works at a hospital, from eleven at night to seven in the morning, at a switchboard. I said that I didn't think they'd appreciate her pink and green hair.

At sixteen years old, Tommy made his way west with his sights set on the growing music scene in Denver, Colorado. There was no plan in place as such, other than to go where the music scene was. As a result, living nomadically and not knowing where he would be sleeping from one night to the next became a norm for Tommy. He recalled in the *Circus* interview:

After they kicked me out of school, there wasn't nothing else for me to do back there. I can't do anything but play guitar. So I moved to Denver and started a band there. We played The Family Dog (nightclub). Luckily we got to play there every week. One night someone from another band heard us play and asked me if I wanted to go to Cincinnati. So I went to Cincinnati. I played with Lonnie Mack. It was a neat place. But it got to the point where, let's see, we played a lot in Louisville, Kentucky. I'd always go down a day earlier to see my friends. I went down and got there about two in the morning, at this restaurant. It was the only place open. I said, 'Hey, does anyone know where I can crash?' Some guy goes, 'Yeah, up the street', so I went up and walked in the room and there was about twenty people lying on the floor, crashed out. I was so tired that I crashed out too. It was about six in the morning and at 10:15 A.M. a cop with a club was beating the bottom of my feet. I was cold, tired and scared. I was sixteen. They checked us all, but found nothing. They arrested me for disturbing the peace. If they want to bust you, they'll bust you. So I was supposed to play that night, but they wouldn't let me make a phone call. Luckily one of the kids got out and called the club and this lady, who owned the club, bailed me out.

A lack of stability and problems with authority became a regular feature in Tommy's life around this time:

I've got arrested for such weird things. When I left Sioux City, for instance, on my first plane ride, me and this friend of mine, Rolland, who got kicked out of school the same time for having a pierced ear, we were sitting on the plane going to Denver and all of a sudden all these cop cars pulled up. I said to Rolland, 'I don't know why, but I think they're coming for us'. What happened was, his mother found a quarter-pound of pot under his bed but burnt it outside before the cops got there, so they didn't have no evidence. So the stewardess said, 'These gentlemen would like to see you'. So they handcuffed us and it was a big, big scene. I was on the third floor and he was on the second of the police station. They asked me what kind of drugs I got and I said I don't got nothing. I didn't know what he was talking about. Then I heard a scream, and I looked out the window and I saw Rolland running out of the building, down the alley, and nobody was chasing him. He got away, hung around downtown Sioux City for three days, hitch-hiked all the way to Seattle, and was there for three months. Then he called me and he goes, 'I'm tired of being on the run', so he hitch-hiked all the way back, went down and says, 'I'm turning myself in'. So the guy goes, 'I can't find your record, could you come back tomorrow?' Me, they put on probation for the year! They said I didn't break the law of the state. They said I broke the law of society for having my hair over my ears. Then in Cincinnati, I was doing acid one night and it started to get light out and I was hitch-hiking and got as far as Junction City, Kansas. At that time my hair was down to here and I had a permanent. I just turned seventeen. I guess hitch-hiking was against the law in that state. The cop said to show him some I.D. I had eight I.D.'s. This was four days after the other bust. We were sleeping under bridges. So I was down at the station for three days. They wouldn't let me make any phone calls. They took me right to the judge. The judge said thirty days in jail. So I was in jail. You just piss all over the floor. One cop felt sorry for me and called my parents. So they sent me down a bus ticket. At one o'clock the guy goes, 'Okay, you can go, your bus is leaving at four o'clock'. He didn't cut my hair, nothing. So they call me out at two o'clock, they knew I was dying to get out of there, and they said the judge said I had to have my hair cut. I said I was leaving, I was leaving their f***ing town, and he said it was either that or thirty days. So they cut my hair off for sanitation. They burned my clothes, cut my hair. I'd had a permanent, so I looked like a little poodle. I took a bus to Sioux City, hung around there, went to Los Angeles, tried to get that band going and ended up pan-handling. The best money I made was pan-handling.

On the image front, Tommy seems to have had the last laugh. In a range of video footage that exists of him, long dyed hair, large earrings and brightly coloured, shiny clothes were not uncommon attire for him. He sometimes wore eye makeup and nail polish, too. His image and his music were both reflective of a very creative human being.

From Tommy's description of his life once he arrived in Denver, even though there were many brushes with the law, there was an innocence about him. A young person trying to find their way in the world while having a strong idea about what he believed in and what he wanted to do. Although Tommy had a hectic start in Denver, arriving there ultimately led him towards the music scene that he was so keen to be a part of from a young age. With his parents' support behind him and with the reasons for his arrest trivial in the grand scheme of things, Tommy was already on the right path that would take him on a journey of meeting other musicians to start building a career with. There is conflicting information making claims about when Tommy started using drugs. I don't think it would do justice to Tommy Bolin's legacy to go into some kind of detailed speculation about the whys, whens and wherefores surrounding which drugs he may or may not have taken at any given time. Drugs may or may not have been a factor with regards to Tommy's arm injury when Deep Purple played in Japan. That holds relevance because of the musical and logistical problems that such injury may have caused to the band at the time. Beyond that, though, this book holds a 'don't gossip' policy.

Tommy was close to his family throughout the dizzying highs and lows of his career. They were supportive and it seems that there was a mutual feeling of joy and appreciation when he returned home as his schedule allowed. It was reported in October 1989 in *Westword:*

Bolin had been playing hard all summer and into the fall (of 1976) when the band finally took two weeks off in late November. The final performance before the break was a welcome home concert in Sioux City, where the Bolin family celebrated the return of its most famous prodigal son.

It was planned that all members of the Tommy Bolin Band would go to their respective homes over the Thanksgiving period and would reunite in Miami for their first gig as the opening act for Jeff Beck. Tommy's brother, Richard, who was eighteen at the time, said, in the same article:

(Thanksgiving was) a whole lot of being with the family, a whole lot of playing and a whole lot of partying. I was in a party stage: we'd go to the local clubs and have fun with the bands on stage. On turkey day, Tommy picked up a stupid old guitar and played songs my dad liked. We were always tight – he loved coming here.

In the article, Richard also expressed his doubts about Tommy's wellbeing at that time. When it was time for Tommy to leave for Miami, he gifted an autographed photo to his parents that read:

To my Mom and Dad who gave me the faith to at least try to make it. And I will for your sake. I love you both so very much. Please don't forget it.

Richard added: 'I think he (Tommy) knew he wasn't coming back'. So, when Richard joked to Tommy not to leave him out, Tommy added to the photo:

Johnny and Ricky, no one had better brothers. I am proud and very lucky for the family of mine.

Poignantly, Richard elaborated:

When he (Tommy) split for the airport, I said 'If I don't see you no more in this world I'll see you in the next and don't be late' he said, 'Ricky, I'm never late'. I knew he was never coming back.

There are other accounts that suggest that Tommy did not anticipate living very long, both from others and the man himself. In the *Tallahassee Democrat* on 8 December 1976, Tommy's road manager, Richard Wood, said that before Bolin's final performance, he had quipped to Wood in an offhand remark:

I want my life to be as exciting as it can possibly be… to die young and to leave behind a good-looking corpse.

It is difficult to comment on this one; life and death and the dark humour that can sometimes be associated with them are so subjective that there's no way of telling how literal Bolin was being when he made this comment. Still, it is interesting to consider that more than one person had a feeling that Bolin was walking a finer line between life and death than perhaps others might have been.

I'm going to conclude this chapter with a quote of Tommy's from October 1976 in *Circus* where he spoke about what kind of pizza he preferred. I accept that it's a very random comment. Why? Because for every syllable spoken about the turbulence of Tommy's short life, it feels right to include just a tiny bit of random human interest too. It's a very 'pop quiz' sort of comment, but still:

The first decent slice of pizza I remember was in the Village, across the street from the Village Gate. I tell you, there's no f***in' place to get decent pizza out here (Los Angeles). There's not enough Italians out here I guess. Even in New York, if you don't get Sicilian, you get the thin pizza. I prefer the Sicilian, maybe because everybody I hang around with is Sicilian. Out here, if they make it, it's all runny. If it's a delivery or something, by the time they get to your house, if you live up a hill or something and there's a bunch of turns, by the time it gets to your house, it all slides across. Maybe they use glue or something in New York.

Also, in the February 1976 Japanese magazine, *Music Life,* Tommy enthused about having been vegetarian for the last five or six years and that even the food on the Japanese part of Deep Purple's tour didn't tempt him otherwise. Tommy spoke with candour and humour in several interviews. In particular, with *7HO Radio Melbourne* on November 26 1975, when asked about his hobbies, he mused:

Music, and drinking, and burning and looting.

Chapter Four: Bolin's Music Before Deep Purple

In all honesty, when it comes to appreciating someone's music, reading an opinion based description of it from any author is hardly going to do it justice. Therefore, please do refer to the discography in the back of this book. A lot of Bolin's music was released after his death. It's remarkable to think that it may not have seen the light of day were it not for him becoming more prominent in the public eye as a result of his presence in Deep Purple. Do refer to the discography here to get the best out of Bolin's music because it really does speak for itself. It's one of those things where (and I'll use a Ritchie Blackmore-related example here because I trust it is likely to be relatable) no matter how eloquently someone describes a song like 'Sixteenth Century Greensleeves', the absolute essence of that song can never be captured with mere words alone. In this same vein, listen to Bolin's music to really get a feel for its character. It is for such reason that this chapter will discuss Bolin's music before *Come Taste The Band*, *Teaser* and *Private Eyes* in a way that is objective in view of Bolin's achievements as a musician rather than function as an analysis of what I think his music sounds like. Listen to it and make up your own mind.

Tommy was active in music by the age of thirteen when he was playing in bands with his peers at high school. Denny And The Triumphs were organised by George Larvick Sr. in 1964. He was the father of bass player George Larvick Jr. and drummer Brad Larvick. When Denny Foote left the band, they renamed in 1965, to Patch Of Blue. The name came from the 1965 film starring Sidney Poitier. Although the band consisted of young teenagers, they were playing at a semi-professional level and George Larvick Sr. managed to get them local gigs as the support act for Herman's Hermits, The Beach Boys and The Animals. Patch Of Blue performed a wide range of musical styles including blues and jazz. It was around this time that Tommy was also playing with South Dakota based band, The Chateaux. In this three-piece group, Tommy played guitar and keyboard.

Leaving home and arriving in Denver by the age of sixteen, Tommy was at a loose end in terms of looking for both somewhere to live and a band to play in. Throughout this time, he was active in jam sessions in the local music scene and it wasn't long before he was asked to join the band, American Standard. Importantly, this was Tommy's introduction to singer Jeff Cook, who would sing and write with Tommy for several years to come. Cook recalled in October 1989 in *Westword*:

American Standard was pretty amateurish, but we were rehearsing in a downtown practice space somewhere on Curtis or Welton, and I heard someone knocking at the door. It was Tommy standing in the snow with his guitar. He said, 'Can I jam?' so we let him in. He plugged in and blew us away.

American Standard became the house band at a nightclub called The Family Dog. It was here that Tommy met his soon-to-be manager, Barry Fey, who managed the club at the time. Subsequently, American Standard felt that they were not moving forward and decided to call it a day. However, Tommy was offered work with a band in Cincinnati. It all fell through though and as a result, by 1968 Tommy was living in Colorado and had formed a new band, Ethereal Zephyr.

Urged to shorten their name to just Zephyr to sound more commercially acceptable, Tommy was moving up in the world in terms of musical opportunities. Zephyr consisted of husband and wife, David Givens on bass and Candy Givens on vocals with Robbie Chamberlin on drums. Tommy's friend Bobby Berge also played drums with the band after Chamberlin left. One of the most memorable aspects of Zephyr is Candy Givens' vocals; they are often considered to be similar to Janis Joplin's – throaty and powerful. Givens' vocal range was vast with a startling mixture of screamingly high notes and very gravelly low notes.

Progress with Zephyr was quick. The band auditioned for Barry Fey in the hope of being offered gigs at Shapes. The nightclub was owned by Fey's friend. Tommy and Fey had already met when Tommy was playing with American Standard at The Family Dog. Zephyr passed their audition with Fey with flying colours and he booked them gigs in other locations where record label bosses would also be present. Fey worked hard when it came to networking on behalf of Tommy, so much so that he remained Tommy's manager from the days of Zephyr right up until his death. More gigs followed and surely enough, record companies began to show interest in Zephyr. A number of bids were made but ultimately, the band signed a contract with Probe, a label under the umbrella of the now-defunct ABC Records. This progression resulted in the band playing an increasing number of venues in a wider range of locations. They were on the same bills as Jethro Tull, Joe Cocker, Janis Joplin, Jimi Hendrix, Mountain, Fleetwood Mac and Led Zeppelin. By the middle of 1969, Zephyr were working on their self-titled first album. It was recorded at Wally Heider Studios in Los Angeles and was produced by Bill Halverson who had already done the sound engineering for bands such as Cream, The Beach Boys and Chuck Berry. As Zephyr were still an up and coming band, their studio time was booked around the timetabling of higher-profile groups. In addition, Zephyr's experience as a live band was such that recording their parts separately in a studio setting was a new challenge for them. David Givens asserted:

We should have made a live record. None of us had been in a studio before, and the producer had no idea what to do with us. I remember Candy singing the same parts forty times and Tommy doing those solos twenty or thirty times in a row.

However, the entire experience was certainly a worthwhile one for Tommy in terms of increasing his profile as a commercial musician. In *The Denver Post* **on 4 January 1970, reporter James Pagliasotti wrote:**

The emergence of Zephyr on the local rock scene could easily be likened to an explosion. It was quick and that emphatic. From the group's tentative formation last January to its rousing performance at the Denver Pop Festival was an evolution of barely five months duration, but it was sufficient to develop what may well be the best rock group ever to come out of Colorado. Ten months ago, Barry Fey, with his characteristic flair for overstatement, told me Zephyr would become a national supergroup within a year. Such, obviously, hasn't been the case. Great groups usually take several years to get it all together, and Colorado isn't the most fertile ground for aspiring musicians. But Zephyr has come a long way in the last year. The group's formation began when guitarist Tommy Bolin and organist John Feris sat in one night with a local group called Brown Sugar. David Givens was playing bass and his wife, Candy, was singing.

In the same review, Bolin was quoted as having said:

Nobody would hire us. I guess we were too far out for them. We played at the Fawcett Room, and several of the Balls for Peace at CU, but not much else. We practised a lot.

Pagliasotti continued:

The practice paid off. Fey was finally persuaded to listen to them and he liked what he heard. He became their business manager, and their fortunes have been on the rise ever since. They have gotten national exposure through appearances at the Avalon in San Francisco, the Whiskey in Los Angeles, and the Boston Tea Party, and have played with The Byrds and Led Zeppelin, among others... Zephyr isn't having much trouble finding work these days, though they still are seldom heard in Colorado. They are booked fairly heavily throughout the next year and will cut their second album sometime in February or March. Meanwhile, local fans had a chance to hear them at the Coliseum last Monday night. From all indications, Zephyr is well on the way to superstar status. They have many things yet to work out, and they must avoid the internal problems that plague so many groups. Assuming they do, they stand a good chance of becoming one of America's premier rock groups, which isn't bad for a band nobody would hire ten months ago.

Zephyr recorded their second album, *Going Back To Colorado*, at Electric Lady Studios in New York and it was released in 1971. By this time the band was under the Warner Brothers record label and the album was produced by Eddie Kramer who had previously worked with Jimi Hendrix and Led Zeppelin. Despite the credibility bestowed by the personnel working on the album, suggesting that Tommy's career was beginning to take off, it was not a commercial success. As a result, Tommy began to look for pastures new once he felt that he had gone as far as he could with Zephyr. Importantly, *Going Back To Colorado* wasn't entirely panned. In the February 1971 *Billboard*, the album was reviewed thus:

Going Back To Colorado gets this new rock group off to a breezy start. The quintet (David and Candy Givens, Bobby Berge, Tommy Bolin and John Faris) has a lot on the ball and they show it off well in songs like 'See My People Come Together', 'Miss Libertine', 'Take My Love' and 'The Radio Song'.

It was also reviewed in February 1971 in *Cash Box*:

It shows they've come a long way since first appearing on the recording scene… (Candy Givens) has, at last, learned how to harness the intense power of her voice. The group's writing has improved considerably also… Tommy Bolin is now writing excellent songs.

It seems that while Zephyr's second album was well received by some, commercially it still wasn't enough to make the band sustainable. Overall, Bolin's time in Zephyr was constructive and pivotal; it gave him more exposure in the music industry at the time. In particular, while Tommy was in New York for the recording of Zephyr's second album, he was active in the music scene there and had already met and played with fusion musicians Jan Hammer and Jeremy Steig. He would be working with them again soon.

After leaving Zephyr, Tommy's musical interests leaned increasingly towards jazz fusion. On such basis, he formed a band called Energy. The band was experimental, and it was never really successful at the time. Jeff Cook said in October 1989 in *Westword*:

Energy played heavy metal jazz fusion – it was just too weird. People wanted to hear Rod Stewart covers; we looked weird and sounded weird.

Nevertheless, Tommy's time in Energy was seemingly constructive for him as a musician on the basis that during this time, he further developed as a performer. In Energy, jazz improvisation and experimentation was very much the order of the day and this is something that Tommy would build on very soon. Energy were not without fans; the band were liked in the small circles of the jazz music scene but this did not bode well commercially. Stanley Sheldon, who played bass in Energy, said this in November 2016 in *Classic Rock*:

> Nobody really understood what we were doing. We were playing in a lot of bars and doing this instrumental fusion music, which no one out there had heard before.

The competitive nature of the music industry combined with the outlandish sound of Energy was such that they were a very short-lived band. They recorded an album but it was not released when Tommy was alive. In an interview in the 1989 documentary, *Tommy Bolin: The Ultimate*, directed by Michael Drumm, Jeff Cook described how Energy came close to scoring a record deal one night when they played in a bar; after the first half of their set, the band celebrated with alcohol when someone from CBS had expressed interest, so much so, that by the second half of their set, they were so inebriated that it made the record executive change their mind about wanting to sign them. In the same documentary, Cook advocated that a strong shared philosophy of Energy was to make music and enjoy making it. Maybe a record deal wasn't the be-all and end-all for the group as a whole, but it put Tommy in an excellent position for further raising his profile within the music community at the time. As ever, Tommy's work with Energy is worth a listen because it demonstrates where he was at creatively prior to taking his career a step further into the area of jazz fusion. Energy's studio recordings from 1972, that were released after he died, are fascinating to listen to. The band had several members come and go in its short lifespan. On some of the recordings, the talents of flautist Jeremy Steig are featured. Some of the longer jams feature more flute solos from Steig than guitar solos from Tommy. This could be of interest to Jethro Tull fans, especially considering that not many rock bands are either willing or able to have a flute player in their ensemble to this day. Cook and Bolin wrote songs that they would also use as material for later projects; the song 'Dreamer' was later used on Tommy's first solo album, *Teaser*. Tommy's work with Energy also informed his writing credits with Deep Purple; the song, 'Lady Luck', which features on the *Come Taste The Band* album, was performed by Bolin in the studio in his days with Energy.

One of Energy's live shows was reviewed in a local music magazine at the time. The review was written by Jon Fosheim. The date of the article is unknown, but the rarity of the review is noteworthy considering that Energy was not a high-profile band. The review stated:

The latest in a series of 'mini-concerts' in Lacotah Hall was performed by Energy Friday night. The usual large crowd of approximately seven hundred people attended. They were not disappointed, as Energy put on perhaps the finest concert of the year, although the acoustics of Lacotah Hall were bad. The group consists of five members, two of whom (Tommy Bolin and Bobby Berge) played with the nationally prominent band, Zephyr until it broke up. Berge and Bolin are both natives of this area, Berge being from Sioux Falls and Bolin from Sioux City. The other three members all hail from Kansas, but the group itself calls Denver its home now. Bolin is considered by many to be one of the finest guitar players in the country, with a versatile expertise in everything from rock and roll to the group's unique style in English blues. His skill does not dominate the group, however, as they do an excellent job of playing as a unit, with Bolin's guitar being neither too loud or too soft. They are especially effective playing the blues, with lead singer Jeff Cook utilising his skill on the harmonica, and keyboard man Tom Stevenson on the electric piano. All material they do is original, except for a couple of the hard-driving, old-time, rock and roll numbers they did Friday night. Energy is currently touring the Mid-west, appearing with such names as It's A Beautiful Day, King Crimson, and Mason Prophet. Their obvious talent has not gone unnoticed; they will be cutting their first album next month.

Of course, Energy weren't given the record deal. This is just one review from a very short period in Tommy's music career. As a result, it wouldn't be realistic to assume that all of Energy's live sets were this well-received (they were, after all, a very short-lived band) but musically, there was certainly a lot of quality content, as is apparent in the posthumous releases listed in the discography of this book. Once again, this is another review that advocated for Tommy's ability to work well as part of an ensemble and shows that he was generous in his sharing of the spotlight.

The next step in Bolin's career was to be far more fruitful. In 1973, Tommy worked on Billy Cobham's album, *Spectrum*. Upon the album's release, it began gaining attention from both the music community and a wider audience. Tommy had done some instrumental sessions with Billy Cobham before receiving a call from him six months later to work on the *Spectrum* album. Seemingly ever humble, in October 1989 in *Westword*, Norma Jean Bell discussed Bolin's disbelief at Cobham's interest in working with him:

He said, 'This guy calls and says this is Billy Cobham and I said, yeah, yeah, yeah, sure this isn't Billy Cobham and hung up'.

As Bolin said in *Melody Maker* in June 1975:

I was starving to death at the time. That album helped me a lot.

Evidently, throughout his career, Bolin was exposed to extremes of both wealth and poverty. In the same interview, he spoke about the differences in working with Cobham and then Alphonse Mouzon:

I also did the *Mind Transplant* album (recorded in 1974) with Alphonse Mouzon. I really like the LP but every tune is about a minute too long. I think the rivalry between Cobham and Mouzon is really funny, but personally I like Billy's drumming more. They play very similarly, but Alphonse has an amazing ego in the first place and Billy plays with more sensitivity. He'd play a country and western tune if you asked him, but Alphonse is more of a lead player.

It is interesting to observe how Bolin was actively involved with so many styles of music in such a short space of time. Alphonse Mouzon's *Mind Transplant* album is jazz fusion orientated as is Billy Cobham's *Spectrum* album. They are certainly stylistically very different from the hard rock music that Tommy was involved with in James Gang. Tommy's versatility in such a short period of time certainly suggests a strong ability to hit the ground running according to the needs of the different artists he worked with, regardless of how involved he was with the writing credits or albums as a whole. On both *Spectrum* and *Mind Transplant* he did not write any of the tracks, it was more of a session musician role for Tommy but certainly, one that helped him gain good publicity as a musician, particularly for his work on *Spectrum*.

It is rumoured that Billy Cobham invited Tommy to tour with him on the basis of his work on the *Spectrum* album but that Tommy opted for working with James Gang because he believed it to be more of an opportunity financially. I am stating this rumour cautiously because looking back at Tommy's work both with Cobham and James Gang respectively, it is of critical acclaim in both cases and with hindsight, who knows which would have been the best career choices for Tommy. It was, after all, Bolin's work on the *Spectrum* album that resulted in him coming to the attention of Deep Purple. By way of context, James Gang's *Bang* album was released in September 1973 and Billy Cobham's *Spectrum* album was released in

October 1973, while James Gang's *Miami* album was released in July 1974. Alphonse Mouzon's *Mind Transplant* album was released in June 1975. As Dave Brown, Bolin's guitar technician at the time pointed out in October 1989 in *Westword*:

> There were people who'd never heard anything about Zephyr or the James Gang, but they knew *Spectrum*.

Later on, Jeff Beck said of *Spectrum* in June 2014 in *Guitar World*:

> Billy Cobham's *Spectrum* album gave life to me at the time. It represented a whole area that was as exciting to me as when I first heard 'Hound Dog' by Elvis Presley. They were inspirational to me to the point that I started to adopt that type of music. Tommy Bolin's guitar playing on *Spectrum* is fantastic.

Cobham was a big deal in the jazz world. He was (and still is) considered by many to be one of the first drummers to combine jazz, funk and rock into a fusion that had more appeal in the mainstream than previous offerings in the same genre from other musicians. It was in 1971 that Cobham co-founded jazz fusion band, the Mahavishnu Orchestra with John McLaughlin. During this time, Cobham became a big name commercially and in 1973, *Spectrum* further elevated his success when he was one of the few drummers to have got a band into the top fifty in the American jazz charts. In an April 2014 interview with *Financial Times*, Cobham mentioned wanting to rebel against the culture at the time of 'drummers need to know their place' in a band. This was a motivating factor in him going on to make *Spectrum*, where he would be in the driving seat. When Tommy Bolin was asked to play on Cobham's *Spectrum* album, he was joining a project with an established musician who knew what he wanted from his band. As a result, *Spectrum* was recorded in just three days. On the album, Cobham's drumming is technically phenomenal and creatively innovative, making this an excellent vehicle through which Tommy was able to showcase his talents on guitar. He had more of a rock music background than the rest of the band who played on the album but this was certainly not to his detriment – it may have even widened the appeal of the album to a number of different audiences. *Spectrum* was reviewed in January 1974 in *Crawdaddy*:

> Pick up on Tommy Bolin's guitar and Lee Sklar's bass pinned down by Cobham's relentless drumming and Jan Hammer's sputtering keyboard. It's simply the best music I've heard in ages.

Tommy's contribution to *Spectrum* was even praised in the August 1974 in *Playboy*:

> Always with one foot firmly planted in Latin rhythm, talented drummer and composer Billy Cobham pivots in a variety of directions with some impressive results. Hard blues in a Latin mode, for instance, comes of a collaboration with guitarist Tommy Bolin and pianist Jan Hammer on *Spectrum* (Atlantic), Cobham's first solo LP. Bolin has Hendrix' technique and a direct feeling for the blues that makes you think of Eric Clapton. Hammer's keyboard work is nothing short of Bachian (sic), ballsy and intergalactic.

In Bolin's solos, he demonstrates a drummer's sense of rhythm. This occurs in many instances on some of the two bar call and response elements of *Spectrum*. In addition to this, Bolin uses a lot of syncopation and improvisation on and around the pentatonic minor scale. This is basically a five-note scale where give or take a bit, it's like playing only black notes on the piano; it's very simple but when done with rhythmic skill and a good feel for the music, it can sound impressive and indeed, beautiful. In an October 1973 issue of *Billboard*, *Spectrum* was reviewed:

> Spectacular is a more apt way to describe the music herein... This is both jazz and contemporary rock with class... Cobham has written all the tunes and they are quite melodic and open to fine improvisations from Joe Farrell on flutes and saxes; Jan Hammer on keyboards and Tommy Bolin and John Tropea on guitars. The latter is played as if it were part of a hard rock group.

It is interesting, and perhaps somewhat ironic, how the reviewer considered that Bolin's contribution to *Spectrum* featured a hard rock emphasis; Bolin was considered too jazz and funk orientated by some of the Deep Purple fans who wanted the band to continue in the direction of hard rock. There's just no pleasing some people! Nevertheless, this was another glowing review for *Spectrum* and indeed Bolin's contribution to it.

Tommy was in James Gang from August 1973 to August 1974. He was recruited to the band to replace guitarist Domenic Troiano. Tommy's songwriting contribution was significant to both albums that he played on with them. Indeed, on the 1973 *Bang* album, he is on the writing credits for eight of the nine songs. He also contributed backing vocals and synthesiser on the album and provided lead vocals on the track 'Alexis'. The band wanted to release 'Alexis' as a single but it was felt by the record company that it would not be a good choice commercially, causing a feeling of frustration amongst the band with regards to this. However, what was apparent is that in terms of writing credits and potential as a solo artist, Tommy was really beginning to come into his own. The same applies to his contribution to his second album with James Gang in 1974, *Miami*. He has writing credits on all ten songs of the album and sang the lead vocal on the track, 'Spanish Lover'. *Bang* was the sixth studio album for James Gang and *Miami* was the seventh. Although the band had an established legacy before Tommy joined, it is evident that the contribution he made to both albums he was involved with was momentous. In February 1974, in the New Mexico State paper *Round Up*, Chuck Wieland reviewed the *Bang* album:

> The James Gang has pulled off its musical resurrection with a *Bang*. Their new album, *Bang*, is the group's best work in many moons. Surviving the departure of guitarist Joe Walsh and the addition of new group musicians is commendable in itself. Any group that can reshuffle its membership and improve itself instantly deserves high praise. On top of all the people problems, the Gang has changed record companies. Guitarist Tommy Bolin has taken over Walsh's duties and had his hands in the writing of all of *Bang's* cuts, minus one. His addition to the Gang has totally obliterated the musical chasm left by Walsh's decision to go solo. Bolin's guitar is tight while being creatively loose.

This is a great review and certainly in praise of what Bolin brought to James Gang when he was recruited as their new guitarist. Many sources, including quotes from Tommy himself, refer to Joe Walsh having left James Gang prior to Bolin joining. In actual fact, it was Domenic Troiano that was the guitarist for James Gang before Bolin joined the band. However, it is Joe Walsh who most often seems to be referred to as the guitarist whose shoes were filled when Bolin joined the band. *Bang* was also reviewed with enthusiasm in December 1973 in *Record World*:

> A rough and raunchy package of heavy metal funk rides in on the James Gang's latest album offering. The gang really cook on 'Must Be Love', 'The Devil Is Singing Our Song' and 'Ride The Wind'.

In February 1974, *Record & Radio Mirror* praised the *Bang* album, as well as Bolin's recruitment to James Gang:

> When Joe Walsh quit the excellent American rock band, it looked like the end. Piffle. In Tommy Bolin, they have found a guitarist and songwriter of equal stature. His playing is seldom boring and often inspired.

In October 1974, *Cash Box* reviewed the James Gang single from the *Miami* album, 'Cruisin' Down The Highway':

> Rock and roll James Gang style has always been a special treat, and this new disc features the Gang at their very best. A catchy riff runs throughout that is a fine undercurrent for some excellent guitar licks by Tommy Bolin. The harmonies are in the James Gang tradition, rounding this record out into the strong rock disk that it is. Watch this cruise up the charts.

When interviewed by *Circus* in October 1976, although Bolin spoke well of the opportunities that being in James Gang provided him with, he was candid about the limitations of being in the band and why he eventually wanted to leave:

> When I got to Los Angeles and was with the James Gang, I got the opportunity to write a lot, to play in front of large audiences, make some money, but it got to a point where I had to leave. The lead singer wanted to do something else, the drummer wanted to be an accountant, the bass player was sick of touring. Then I joined another band, then I took the year off to look for a lead singer, I spent money, and threw it away. Then I ran out of money. I said, 'f*** it, I'm going to do it myself', and so I did. I got a contract and then I got an offer to play with Deep Purple.

Bolin said in June 1975 in *Melody Maker*:

> With the James Gang, it got kind of tedious, playing the same things every night, and there was never any close communication between us, on stage or off and people in the audience could feel that.

Jeff Cook discussed how he believed that Tommy wasn't happy in James Gang in the October 1989 in *Westword*:

> I don't think he felt he had the freedom to do what he wanted, but it was a lot of money. It was just a great opportunity. The idea down the road was to put Energy back together.

This comment of Cook's is interesting in that it implied that while Bolin was willing to make career decisions that had financial and commercial benefit, the need to be true to what he wanted to do musically was never far away. In the same article, David Givens said:

> When we met Tommy, 'commercial' was a joke. When he told me he was going

to play with the James Gang, I laughed. We used to use them as an example of what we didn't want to be. But he had just made *Spectrum* and he was really proud of that. At that point there wasn't a whole lot going on, he wanted the good life.

In February 1976 in *Rolling Stone*, Bolin discussed his decision to leave James Gang, stating that it was no longer a learning process.

The theme that Tommy was often a replacement for other musicians was apparent in the media even before the Deep Purple episode of his career. In January 1974, *Cash Box* ran a story about how, for the cover of the James Gang album, *Bang*, Tommy's face was airbrushed onto a photograph of the band that had been taken before he joined it. The validity of this story, I think, is debatable. Given the limited technology at the time, whoever's job it was to do that did an outrageously good job of it! Also, there are no other strong sources that corroborate the story, so I'd recommend caution with regards to its believability. However, either way, what is significant about this story is that the media account of it is reflective of a theme that may have haunted Tommy throughout significant parts of his career. *Cash Box* reported that the *Bang* album cover:

… depicts four members of the group and one girl all huddled together looking over other album covers… Joe Walsh's picture has been airbrushed out and 'new edition to the act' Tommy Bolin's image is inserted.

Bang reached number 122 in the American charts and *Miami* got to number 97. Bolin's performance with James Gang was often appreciated in a positive light. In March 1974 in *Record & Radio Mirror*, reporter Barry Taylor reviewed Tommy's performance from a show at the New York Academy of Music:

Back to the Academy on Sunday Night, the new James Gang with guitarist Tommy Bolin put on a high energy display, drawing most of their material from the latest album, *Bang*. Lead singer Roy Kenner has a sure strong voice, but his between-song raps that scolded the audience for not getting out of their seats and dancing in the aisles was idiotic and totally uncalled for, especially in the uptight Academy of Music. The ushers constantly look like they fear the revolution that's about to erupt at any second. Otherwise, the James Gang showed what is perhaps their tightest combination yet; Jim Fox still mixes jazz and rock drumming with technical flair while bassist Dale Peters works off him like a well-oiled machine. Bolin (who survived the 60's practically unrecognised with the underrated group, Zephyr) earned kudos only after his work on Billy Cobham's *Spectrum* album. He fits into the James Gang like a hand in a glove. Their music always focused on the pyrotechnics of their guitarists – from Joe Walsh to Domenic Troiano, and Bolin could be the best one yet. He has a fluent style which commands your attention, and yet doesn't detract from Fox and Peters. His use of electronic gadgets, which at times gave the guitar a synthesised effect was done with taste.

The *Miami* album was reviewed in August 1974 in *Billboard*:

Good, basic hard rock has always been the forte of the James Gang and they have refined that format to near perfection here. Nothing pretentious, just the rough but controlled lead vocals of Roy Keener and the chugging guitars of Tommy Bolin which result in a mix of the material we commonly hear on FM radio and the AM commercial hits. Cuts are the kind one can enjoy without analysing, and when you get down to it, that is what rock is all about. The best cuts are 'Cruisin' Down The Highway', 'Sleepwalk', 'Praylude/Red Skies' and 'Head Above The Water'.

Musically and commercially, a review such as this suggests that there may have been more mileage for Bolin in staying with James Gang for longer. But clearly, from a range of sources, he didn't want to.

Having established his reputation through his work on Billy Cobham's *Spectrum* album, Tommy was invited to play on Alphonse Mouzon's album, *Mind Transplant*. It was recorded over five sessions in December 1974 and was released in March 1975 on the famous Blue Note jazz label. Even after Billy Cobham's *Spectrum* album, albums by solo drummers were still a commercial risk due to the possibility that they might only be popular amongst a smaller audience. Nevertheless, Alphonse Mouzon's *Mind Transplant* album is certainly not without merit. As with his work with Billy Cobham, Bolin approached the written musical score with minimal engagement due to his inability to read music. The result was beautiful, however. Throughout the *Mind Transplant* album, Bolin demonstrates his talents as an improviser who can feel the mood of the music and work within the structure of it harmoniously. Not only does his work enhance what the other musicians are doing, it sparkles in its own right. The structured element of the composition was created entirely by Alphonse Mouzon. His recruitment of a range of talented musicians resulted in an album that is full of interesting melodic ideas and catchy rhythmic structures. *Mind Transplant* is an interesting example of jazz fusion that embraces elements of rock and funk. Not only was Tommy Bolin a part of this, but his contribution to this album is significant and it really showcases his talent, both generally and in the context of the genre. On 18 May 2011 in an interview with *Something Else*, Alphonse Mouzon talked about Bolin's contribution:

> He (Bolin) made that record, along with Lee Ritenour. There were actually three guitars, with Jay Graydon. I heard Bolin on the *Spectrum* record and I wanted him on guitar. We had met before when we sat in back in Boulder in 1974. I had the night off and sat in. So when I went back to New York and heard *Spectrum*, I had to have him. That was great. I just let him stretch.

By this point in Bolin's career, he was becoming a popular choice of session musician on the merit of his previous work. *Mind Transplant* was reviewed favourably in March 1975 in *Cash Box*:

> Alphonse Mouzon has made his third album as a leader and it is a progressive rock record of the highest quality. The music revolves around the guitar and Mouzon's drums. Though it may shock many to hear it, many of Mouzon's solo riffs sound like Billy Cobham's. Light rapid fluttering notes bounce from the drumsticks in long paradiddle rolls. Tommy Bolin and Lee Ritenour are the primary guitarists and their parts are characteristic of rock music. Their solos are tasteful and intelligent though they tend at times to be repetitious.

Tommy received much critical acclaim for his work on the Moxy album in 1975. The story of how he came to play on the album is one of being in the right place at the right time. He was brought in to solo on six of the eight songs on the album because he happened to be in the studio next door to the band at Sound City Studios in California. Moxy's manager, Roland Paquin, knew Tommy from when he had been the road manager for James Gang when Tommy was their guitarist. The album was a relatively high-profile project because the band were on the Polydor label, having recently signed a contract with them. By the time Tommy came to play with Moxy, the band already had a rich history. Formed in Toronto, Canada in 1974, the singer Douglas 'Buzz' Sherman had already enjoyed a reasonably successful career (including a single in the top thirty) since 1967, in a band called Leigh Ashford. Moxy also included members who had previously been in another group from Toronto called Outlaw Music. The band's members were drummer Billy Wade, bassist Terry Juric and guitarist Earl Johnson. Both Wade and Johnson had played with Sherman in Leigh Ashford.

The connections between the members of Moxy had already been established. Moxy, as a band built on established musicians and personnel dynamics, were gaining more commercial momentum. This was an excellent project for Tommy to be part of; it offered him further exposure as an excellent musician in his own right. The 'Can't You See I'm a Star' track from the Moxy album was released as a single in 1974 on Yorkville Records and although Bolin did not solo on this track (the guitar solo was provided by Eric Johnson), it added to the profile of the band, getting the exposure that would help put Tommy in a favourable light. More importantly, perhaps, Tommy played the guitar solo on the song that was released on the B-side of the 'Can't You See I'm a Star' single. The B-side track that features Tommy's solo is called 'Out Of The Darkness'.

Meanwhile, tracks from the Moxy album were getting a lot of airplay on American FM radio stations. By this point, Tommy's participation in the album was such that it helped to promote it. People were interested in his work and he was becoming a bigger deal commercially with each project he embraced. Bolin only played on Moxy's first album, but he was certainly part of something important. It was suggested in November 1976 in *Billboard,* that the Moxy album that Bolin was part of was pivotal for the band overall:

> This group has built a following on the strength of its last LP and delivers a strong second effort with this one.

From leaving home and heading for Denver at the age of sixteen, Tommy Bolin was constantly active as a musician. Sometimes he was struggling for money and commercial success looked doubtful. At other times he was working with some very high-profile people in the industry and was enjoying the pay and the recognition that came with that territory. There were seemingly a lot of ups and downs but one thing remains consistent – Bolin never stopped making music. He never stopped exploring a variety of many new projects that spanned a range of musical styles. He developed his craft and worked hard. He showed himself to be capable of diversity and adapting to the needs of other bands, musicians, producers and live audiences. Between leaving home and joining Deep Purple in 1975, Tommy Bolin had done the foundation work for his musical career – and then some. The history of Tommy's formative years is often overlooked in his legacy. For many, it remains either ignored or perhaps of less interest because it took place before he got his big break (in commercial terms at least) with Deep Purple. But still, Billy Cobham's *Spectrum* album was a highlight of Tommy Bolin's career, as was his work in Zephyr, not to mention his work in James Gang, and with Moxy, and Alphonse Mouzon. Essentially, there were many highlights of exciting, pivotal and crucial projects in Bolin's career even before Ritchie Blackmore had left Deep Purple. Of course, all these projects resulted in varying levels of commercial success but the point is this: Tommy

Bolin was an established musician long before he had the misfortune of being berated by many Deep Purple fans purely for not being Ritchie Blackmore.

MIAMI WAS A QUIET PLACE...

UNTIL THE JAMES GANG ARRIVED.

Palm trees swayed and graceful flamingoes toppeled when Roy Kenner,
Tommy Bolin, Dale Peters and Jimmy Fox strode into Miami's Criteria
studio to record their new Atco album.
But as they started laying down the tracks, Miami started to rock and roll
to their dynamic, energy packed music.
And now Miami will never be the same.

**"Miami." From The James Gang.
On Atco records and tapes.**
Produced by The James Gang and Tom Dowd.

Left and above: Two adverts promoting the James Gang albums *Bang* and *Miami*.

Chapter Five: Come Taste The Band

Deep Purple's *Come Taste The Band* album was released in October 1975. All pains and frustrations of dealing with the nightmares of the tour were yet to happen – it began in the November. This makes it entirely plausible that creating the album itself may have been a positive experience for Bolin and the rest of Deep Purple. In his interview in November 1975 with *Creem* magazine, Bolin expressed much enthusiasm for the project:

Between the Purple and the solo stuff, I couldn't be happier. I feel I can finally try all the things I've always wanted to do. It's like a new lease on life.

Also, despite the demise of morale throughout the tour for *Come Taste The Band*, the album itself did receive some very positive reviews around that time. In February 1976, *Rolling Stone* advocated:

The album takes off in the chunky funk-rock style of Purple's last two albums. Distinctions don't develop until the material becomes familiar. Like Blackmore, Bolin establishes tension between Purple's solid rhythm foundation and his own sustained clarity and agitated upper-fret playing. While Blackmore was largely confined by this style, Bolin employs it as only one of many. His more flexible approach to writing and arranging produces a more melodic and dynamic feel. With him, Purple's music has outgrown the predictability of the past. Textures replace a reliance on volume, and changes in tone and pace more frequently contrast and augment each other. There is evidence of give and take that Deep Purple hasn't shown for some time. David Coverdale's emerging songwriting talents combine with Bolin's in 'Dealer'. Lord's more sophisticated keyboard work surfaces in several tunes. A visible attempt to experiment has expanded the group's music beyond the heavy-metal trap, and this could lead them to rediscover the progressive style that somehow vanished after *In Rock*.

The review of *Come Taste The Band* in *Rolling Stone* is reflective of what can be enjoyed about Bolin's recruitment to Deep Purple; it was an exciting new opportunity to bring some fresh innovation to the band - in the same way that the 1970 *Deep Purple In Rock* album with Mk2 of the band was so musically refreshing and stylistically very different to the three previous albums that had been made by Mk1. Frustratingly, other reviews of *Come Taste The Band* fixated on the departure of Blackmore from the lineup. In November 1975 in *Billboard*, *Come Taste The Band* received a mixed review. While the reviewer considered the merits of the album, there was still a complaint that Bolin was not Blackmore:

First set from the long-standing heavy metal band with new guitarist Tommy Bolin is a better than average set of hard rock, but somehow lacks the drive the band enjoyed under the guidance of Ritchie Blackmore. Still, with Jon Lord working his patented keyboards and David Coverdale on vocals, the LP should satisfy dyed in the wool Purple fans. Some good instrumental work here as well as the rock and roll singing. Frenetic material works best. The best cuts are 'Lady Luck', 'I Need Love', 'Drifter', 'This Time Around' and 'Owed To G'.

What a strange review! The reviewer complained about Bolin not being Blackmore and yet, every single song that the reviewer listed as a highlight is on the album directly because of Bolin. He has writing credits on all of them and 'Lady Luck' is on the album due to Bolin's connection to Jeff Cook. Ridiculous! Another example of the media choosing to negate Bolin's recruitment to Deep Purple while not really taking account of the extent of his contribution to the Mk4 lineup. Hughes said of 'I Need Love' in his autobiography:

I like this song. Tt had that Motown groove to the drums. It's very Tommy; it's what he was all about

And of 'Drifter':

A good song. It could have been on a James Gang album, guitar-wise.

And of 'Owed To G':

'Owed To G' was just Tommy, and his ode to Gershwin.

To get the most enjoyment out of the *Come Taste The Band* album, it seems imperative to appreciate it as a fresh piece of work in its own right rather than expecting it to be a rigid continuation of the music that Deep Purple made with Ritchie Blackmore, even so far as the two Mk3 albums, *Burn* and *Stormbringer* both released in 1974. Bolin told Geoff Barton in September 1975:

The new album is more sophisticated than the old Purple stuff, but I don't think that'll matter. The kids are more clued-in than they were a year ago, so I think it'll be accepted. Highly. Very highly. During Ritchie's last days with the band, most of the members were so f***ed off with everything. I think bringing in a new guitar player has made a hell of a difference. I honestly believe that we should keep some connections with the past, not sever them all, but at the same time begin to progress in our own direction.

The *Come Taste The Band* album certainly does stand up in its own right, and essentially, it is a predominant aspect of Tommy's musical legacy.

Having undergone the audition process at Pirate Sound Studios, the band stayed there throughout June and early July 1975 as they began writing and rehearsing for the album that would become *Come Taste The Band*. Tommy's songwriting talents were such that, as with when he was in James Gang, he brought a wealth of material with him; a backlog of songs that he had written that were yet to see the light of day, and sadly, many of which may never. It is certainly no coincidence that Tommy has writing credits on seven of the nine songs on *Come Taste The Band*. The song 'Lady Luck' was written by Jeff Cook from Tommy's time in Energy. David Coverdale shares a writing credit on this song as he reworked it for Deep Purple. As was common with the recording process at the time, tapes were reused and countless performances were lost, the exception being a few that were transferred to cassette. The surviving material was released as *Days May Come And Days May Go: The California Rehearsals* and *1420 Beachwood Drive: The California Rehearsals Part Two* in 2000 on Purple Records. Tommy's performances on these recordings were played with passion and enthusiasm.

Towards the end of July, it was necessary for Tommy to depart to go to The Record Plant in Los Angeles to begin working on his solo album, *Teaser*. He was already contractually committed to this project, as was acknowledged by Deep Purple when they welcomed him into the band. Despite this, in Geoff Barton's August 2017 article in *Classic Rock*, Jon Lord was quoted posthumously:

Tommy's solo career was nascent, as it was his actually joining Purple that kick-started *Teaser*. I don't think he was front-page news. Certainly, in the music community he was, everybody recognised him as a young whiz kid, but he was pretty much unknown to the public at large. Still, I can understand why there might've been a bit of tension within Purple concerning Tommy's, shall we say, extracurricular activities.

In the same article, Glenn Hughes said:

I can't lie to you; it (Tommy's solo project) was a slight problem. It might've been more on the management side of things. Tommy had his own manager, a tough guy, a hardhead from Denver called Barry Fey. He was a real old-school, Peter Grant type. I think the management of Purple definitely had problems with that.

Dave Brown, Bolin's guitar technician at the time, discussed the implications of

Tommy having to juggle two major recording projects. He said in October 1989 in *Westword:*

> It started as an obligation, but we enjoyed it, being able to run to London to mix *Teaser* and then to Germany to do *Come Taste The Band*.

Come Taste The Band was recorded in the August and September of 1975 when Tommy returned from his solo project to work with Deep Purple at Musicland Studios in Munich. It was engineered by Martin Birch who had worked with Deep Purple since their earlier days on *Concerto For Group And Orchestra* in 1969. Deep Purple is also credited for their sound engineering work on *Come Taste The Band*. By early October, Tommy had finished recording material in New York for his *Teaser* album at Electric Lady Studios. He then went to Trident Studios in London to do some final work on it. Tax restrictions had made Deep Purple reluctant to participate on the album. Although Glenn Hughes chose not to be credited for it at the time, he contributed vocals on the track, 'Dreamer'. Deep Purple returned to Pirate Sound Studios in mid-October in order to get ready for touring the album. It would seem that June and July was, musically, a positive experience for Tommy with Deep Purple because he had a lot of creative freedom to bring his own ideas in and to be celebrated for what he was bringing to the table. Glenn Hughes recalled in his autobiography:

> So we're back in Musicland in Germany to record the album. We're a new band again and we've been invigorated by Tommy, because of his childlike qualities and the fact that he wasn't a Blackmore clone.

By October, however, Bolin was probably starting to feel the toxicity of being Ritchie Blackmore's replacement in a way that threatened to negate his own talents. He was expected to learn Blackmore's guitar parts note for note in order to comply with a setlist that featured Deep Purple's older material with Blackmore. Understandably, this could have been a notable factor in affecting morale. In particular, it may even have been outside of what Bolin's expectations were when he joined Deep Purple. In July 1975, David Coverdale had told *Sounds*:

> We haven't discussed what we're gonna be playing in the (live) set yet. We'll wait before the album comes out before we do a tour. So when we actually present Tommy on stage the people in the audience are gonna know what he sounds like because they'll already have heard the album.

With this in mind, what Tommy said in March 1976 in *Record Mirror & Disc* doesn't seem unreasonable:

They (Deep Purple) gave me the tapes of the old band, and I threw them away. I can do a few things like 'Smoke On The Water' but didn't want to do things the way they were. I'm happier the way things are now. I didn't even want to listen to those things because I thought it might influence me subconsciously.

The making of _Come Taste The Band_ was certainly not plain sailing. The design of Musicland recording studio in Munich was such that the studio was situated under the Arabella Hotel where the band was staying throughout the recording process. Although this set-up had an element of convenience to it, it was also a prominent factor in contributing to the building tensions and difficulties within the band. The lack of personal space between colleagues was such that each member of the band became more exposed to each other's problems at the time. Both Bolin and Hughes were in the depths of their drug problems throughout their residence in Munich. In the August 2017 issue of _Classic Rock_, Geoff Barton quoted Hughes from an earlier interview:

Tommy had big bag of blow flown in from Boulder, Colorado. I got a key from the manager of the hotel and went into Tommy's room and found the stash. I dipped into the bag and took a couple of grams out of it, but after a line or two in my room, I felt so guilty. I called (personal assistant) Nicky Bell and gave it back to him. Then I had a bit of a meltdown. Cocaine psychosis took over – it's a condition similar to paranoid schizophrenia. I freaked out. I rugby-tacked Nicky Bell in the lobby of the hotel and hit him. I also attacked another member of our crew, Ossy Hoppe, in front of paying customers in a restaurant. The next thing I knew I was on the plane home. The only way they could stop me going crazy was to send me back to England. I was ill and needed to be taken care of by a doctor. Other people were having their own problems with their own demons – wine, women, gambling, whatever. They had their own secrets. Some people were drinking too much, some people were smoking dope.

In the same article, Barton quoted Jon Lord from a previous interview:

Everybody sniffed a bit of coke in those days. People were almost doing it in restaurants, it was that prevalent. It was no big deal as far as I was concerned. But with Glenn, it was obvious that he was on a downward spiral. Then I became aware that Tommy was right there with him. Indeed, they were both having the times of their lives. Or so they thought. But what I didn't know was that Tommy also had a problem with heroin.

With Hughes sent home to England, there was still work to be done and Tommy was given the responsibility of playing bass on parts of _Come Taste The_

Band when Hughes was unavailable to do it. Tommy also contributed some of the vocals on the track 'Dealer'.

Despite all of the issues during the making of *Come Taste The Band*, there really is no denying the positive reviews that the album received. Geoff Barton reviewed it in October 1975 in *Sounds:*

> Tommy Bolin has injected a heavy dose of fresh energy. I haven't heard Purple play with such boyish enthusiasm in a long time. His guitar work is succinct, immensely fluid but never overbearing. Indeed, **Come Taste The Band** displays a much freer, give-and-take musical attitude than even several early Purple albums.

In 2010, The 35th Anniversary Edition of *Come Taste The Band* was released as a double CD set. It features some recordings that were previously considered to have been lost; a single edit and remastered versions of 'You Keep On Moving' and remixed tracks by Kevin Shirley of Aerosmith, 'Same in LA' and 'Bolin/ Paice Jam'. Glenn Hughes was actively involved with the project and indeed, has been instrumental with keeping Tommy's legacy alive today. Hughes has attended, and performed at, a number of Tommy Bolin tribute concerts. It could be the case that the tour with Deep Purple was what challenged Bolin more than the creation of the *Come Taste The Band* album. Certainly, the intensity of dealing with audience heckles and expectations to play Blackmore era Deep Purple songs exactly the same as Blackmore can't have helped Tommy's live performance. This review of *Come Taste The Band* in March 1976 in *Circus* could certainly be reflective of the possibility that it wasn't until the live tour that things started to unravel:

> If the Blackmore daze (sic) are gone, it's just something we're going to have to forget – or at least remember only when listening to the old LPs. Bolin is clearly in control now, having written or collaborated on all nine tracks of **Come Taste the Band**, thereby taking over another position Blackmore held so dear, that of chief composer. Even though the whole band makes the music, the spotlight will be on the guitar player. And most of the pressure. But if this album is any indication, we're going to be getting a lot tougher records from the new Deep Purple.

Come Taste The Band, regardless of whether or not it should have been labelled as a Deep Purple album, is a great album in and of its own right. It is the product of what happens when five brilliantly talented musicians collaborate creatively. I recently managed to get hold of an original songbook of the sheet music for the album, published by Warner Bros. in 1976. For the age of the book, it's in outrageously good condition. I sourced it from a house clearance somewhere in America. It blows my mind that it was probably just sitting there for years and I was fascinated to see some of the intense technicality of songwriting that is present. For instance, the riff on 'Love Child' is in 7/4 time – most of the song is in common time except for that riff. That's some pretty complex writing there as 7/4 is an immensely unusual choice of time signature in the context of many musical genres. Equally, 'Owed To G' is in 12/8 time. While the use of complex or unusual time signatures is certainly not a prerequisite for music to be considered of good quality, *Come Taste The Band* features a diverse range of creativity and despite the problems that Deep Purple experienced during the recording of the album, there is so much there that really is worth listening to. *Come Taste The Band* does not sound like the output of a group who were grudgingly going through the motions. We may never know how the individuals concerned were really feeling during the making of the album, but I think it is of massive importance to appreciate *Come Taste The Band* for what it actually sounds like rather than the associated baggage surrounding it that all too often overshadows it. The potential for success was there in the Mk4 lineup of Deep Purple. The talent was certainly there. Musically, the *Come Taste The Band* album itself is not particularly reflective of a band that is unhappily falling apart. There is a great sadness in that with regards to what could have been – it is the cruel nature of speculation and hindsight I suppose. In reality, clashes in musical interests, drug abuse problems and of course, egos, were such that the Mk4 lineup of Deep Purple never really had the chance to capitalise on the talent they had as an ensemble.

It is certainly fascinating to wonder what a second album by this lineup would sound like had things not gone so chronically wrong in so many ways. Frustratingly, it does feel like many fans are keen to deny the presence of *Come Taste The Band* as part of Deep Purple's true legacy on the basis that it wasn't, for example, *Deep Purple In Rock* (1970) or *Machine Head* (1972). They are both great albums – monumentally essential listening. But in reality *Come Taste The Band* was reflective of what all bands eventually go through – change. The album often divides the opinion of Deep Purple fans in an absolute way; it is seemingly either loved or hated. Musically though, it really does have a lot going for it. Bolin's guitar performance is spot on. There's no real fault in it and as ever, Lord, Paice, Coverdale and Hughes played just as well as they had done in earlier Deep Purple albums. The sound that Deep Purple fans had become accustomed to from the likes of *Deep Purple In Rock* and *Machine Head* is absolutely spellbinding. Arguably, nothing like them really existed before. While *Come Taste The Band* perhaps doesn't have the shock value of those albums, it is certainly worthwhile both as a great album in itself and as part of Deep Purple's and Tommy Bolin's legacy.

The extent to which the quality of *Come Taste The Band* is perhaps negated and overshadowed by the problems Deep Purple had with doing the tour for the album is evident in Peter Crescenti's review of their gig at Radio City Music Hall, New York in February 1976 in *Sounds*:

Taste The Band (sic) album, ironically one of Purple's best but which is now skidding down the charts as quickly as the band seem to be stumbling towards oblivion. Purple's energy, it seems, is being devoured by the compromises and concessions that have to be made by their two singers David Coverdale and bassist Glenn Hughes. In accommodating Hughes' desire to sing more (which still isn't enough to satisfy him anyways) lead singer Coverdale has to leave the stage three or four times a set, for a total of about thirty minutes, a disaster for a performer like Coverdale whose most immediate concern is establishing a rapport. It is also rumoured that some members of the band have become disillusioned with Tommy Bolin's solo ambitions as his *Teasers* (sic) album shoots up the charts while Purple's drops. Bolin seems to sense that the end of the band may be near and his playing on stage reflects that attitude much of the time. The audience at Radio City seemed to sense this too and reacted with the frenzy typical of Purple fans only when favourites like 'Smoke On The Water' were offered. It would be unfortunate if the band were to fall apart, especially of the promise of their last album. Purple occasionally flashed the brilliance that they were more than capable of but considering the divided loyalties that have splattered within the band, they might just be better off packing it in.

Left and below Two adverts promoting Tommy's studio album with Deep Purple, *Come Taste The Band*.

Chapter Six: Teaser

Tommy Bolin's stint in Deep Purple was undeniably a boost for the marketing of his *Teaser* album. So much so in fact, that when the *Teaser* LP was released, it had a sticker on it stating the Tommy was the guitarist with Deep Purple. The *Teaser* album came out pretty much around the same time that *Come Taste The Band* did (17 November 1975 and 10 October 1975 respectively). Some accounts say that this added to the tensions within Deep Purple at the time, but others advocate that because Tommy had secured his solo record deal prior to joining Deep Purple, it is not as if *Teaser* was ever a surprise. Deep Purple knew about it from their first meeting with Tommy. A rumour exists that Tommy's solo deal had initially been offered to him by Atlantic but when Tommy's manager Barry Fey insisted that it would be him who would ultimately choose the producer for the album, Atlantic scrapped the deal. By this time Tommy had already made a decent amount of demos and was able to secure a recording contract with Nemperor Records in April 1975. The head of Nemperor Records, Nat Weiss, was a friend of Fey.

By this point, Tommy had several musicians in his network and as a result, he had a good range of contacts to assist in choosing who he wanted to play on the record. So much so that each track on *Teaser* consists of a different lineup. Bobby Berge who had played with Tommy in Energy and Zephyr was present for the sessions for the track 'Lotus'. Stanley Sheldon (best known for playing bass with Peter Frampton) played bass on most of the tracks on the album. Bolin had previously worked with Jan Hammer during the sessions for Billy Cobham's *Spectrum* album, so Hammer played the drums on the track, 'People, People'. Drummer Prairie Prince played on the tracks 'Wild Dogs' and 'Savannah Woman'. He had met Tommy in Phoenix when he had been in the opening band for Zephyr and Jethro Tull one night. Once the recording sessions were taking place at Trident Studios in London, Phil Collins (of Genesis fame) played drums on 'Savannah Woman'. Jeff Porcaro (of Toto fame) played drums on the tracks, 'Teaser', 'Dreamer' and 'Homeward Strut'. David Foster, who played keyboards for the tracks, 'The Grind', 'Dreamer' and 'Homeward Strut', eventually went on to be a vice president at Atlantic Records. Clearly, there was a wealth of talented people keen to work with Tommy on the *Teaser* album. This speaks volumes about the momentum that Tommy's career was starting to gain by that point. The album is still cohesive in terms of Tommy's songwriting, guitar playing and vocals, despite utilising the talents of many musicians and covering a range of musical styles including hard rock, reggae, Latin and jazz. *Teaser* was recorded at a number of studios; The Record Plant in Los Angeles in July 1975, Electric Lady Studios in New York in the September and in October at Trident Studios in London.

It was during the June of the earliest sessions for *Teaser* that Bolin was invited to join Deep Purple. Despite his passion for his solo career and the way that his debut album was taking shape, the offer to join a big-name band like Deep Purple was too good to miss. Tommy was only aware of a few of Deep Purple's songs when he was invited to audition with them but still, it was a good opportunity commercially. Bolin's guitar technician at the time, Dave Brown, talking to *Westword* in October 1989, said:

> Deep Purple came out of nowhere. Tommy already felt so good about his own thing and he auditioned almost as a lark.

I can see why it could be perceived as being insulting to Deep Purple but equally, if you're invited to audition with one of the highest-profile bands in the world, maybe keeping a sense of humour about the whole thing helps maintain a sense of calm and reality about the surreal nature of the situation. It's an interesting approach for any audition really. There's no point going in so serious that you're petrified of not getting the gig through having put the opportunity on a pedestal. After joining Deep Purple, the recording of *Teaser* was put on hold. This eventually led to Tommy juggling two major projects concurrently. Consequently, he was forced to pause his solo career due to commitments with Deep Purple. His scope for *Teaser* promotional touring was also compromised.

With *Come Taste The Band* and *Teaser* released almost simultaneously, there are two possible ways of looking at this. Firstly, there may have been a conflict of interest and a fear of one album overshadowing the other. Deep Purple certainly had more promotional power behind them. Alternatively, with both albums coming out at the same time, one might promote the other and may have turned Deep Purple fans on to Bolin's music and Bolin's fans on to Deep Purple's music. It is generally agreed across all accounts – including interviews with both Deep Purple Mk4 members and Bolin himself – that Bolin received a very different reception from America than he did from British audiences. Although the taunts of 'Where's Ritchie?' were not exclusive to Britain, it certainly seems that this is the part of the tour where they were more apparent.

Tommy already had more of a following in America due to all of his musical projects before Deep Purple having taken place there. Essentially, America was Bolin's home ground. All that said, when Deep Purple had disbanded in March 1976, Bolin needed to get things rolling again in America with regards to promoting his solo career. Tracks from the *Teaser* album had been given FM radio play; in April 1976, *Cash Box* advocated of the single, 'Savannah Woman', 'Look for this one to show up on FM lists'. In April 1976, *Record World* reviewed it too:

The mambo like rhythms of this record, show a side of Bolin that doesn't surface with Deep Purple. A tasteful performance by all makes this an appealing item.

Additionally, in December 1975, *Cash Box* had suggested that the tracks 'Teaser' and 'Marching Powder' were worthy of AM play. Bolin was becoming well known, but inevitably, he had still not been able to give his solo career and indeed the *Teaser* album the attention that he had intended to at the start of the project before Deep Purple had come into the picture. It wasn't until after his time with Deep Purple that Bolin was able to put all of his energy into his solo career. In the *Good Times* newspaper in February 1976, *Teaser* was reviewed as follows:

Teaser shows that his (Bolin's) stay with Purple will be brief – there's no way he can be in a band without being its leader. The album is eclectic, ranging from ballad to scorcher with Bolin searching for a sound that can be totally his own. His instrumentals are striking, but his vocals are weak. He should either find another singer or go totally instrumental like Jeff Beck, for Bolin possesses the talent to equal ***Blow By Blow*** (Jeff Beck's second solo album, released in March 1975). 'Marching Powder' is Mahavishnuized (sic) with former McLaughlin drummer Michael Waldon supplying a sturdy bottom, while 'Homeward Strut' is a synthesised number. The rest of the tracks feature Tommy's vocals but only the opening 'The Grind' employs any backing vocals (The Sniffettes) over Bolin's sliding, slashing guitaring. For the most part, his vocals are not strong enough to bear the weight of the musicianship. 'Teaser' is a smashing bone crusher done in a trio format; the others all employ between four and seven musicians. 'People, People' has an unusual funkiness (though it has no soul), keyboarded, drummed and synthesised by Jan Hammer and horned by David Sanborn. And 'Wild Dogs' is an overdubbed race of guitars displaying concepts that are sure to be expanded upon the next LP. Two songs stand out for their mellower tones. 'Dreamer' is dynamic in its multi-textures and tempo changes which build quickly to a climax while the Latin influenced 'Savannah Woman' is lyrical with guest underpinnings from Tubes skin man Prairie Prince. These songs show that there are many sides of Bolin that easily can be developed later. *Teaser* lives up to its title: It's enticing yet not magnetic. *Teaser*, however, offers a lot – maybe too many styles but it's only the beginning of an all-important solo career. Here's hoping Bolin doesn't waste his time in Purple – *Teaser's* impact greatly exceeds ***Come Taste The Band***.

What a fascinating review! It is great to see that Tommy's solo work was being appreciated as something of a vehicle that would ultimately allow him to leave Deep Purple behind. Anyone wanting to champion Tommy Bolin as the underdog of Deep Purple Mk4 can take something positive from this review of *Teaser*. To compare *Come Taste The Band* with *Teaser* seems futile due to how musically different the two are for a variety of reasons; stylistically they are very different because, with Deep Purple, Bolin was joining an established act that already had their own baggage, brand and expectations. With *Teaser*, Tommy was very much in the driving seat and it is fantastic to think that his talent was given a means through which to be embraced in its own right. Tommy was treated as a replacement in James Gang and Deep Purple, despite the strong contributions he made to all related albums, so *Teaser* seems to signify the start of a new beginning. Commercially, this could have been an exciting time for Tommy and his supporters. The reviewer makes comments that imply that the *Teaser* album features a range of musical styles and influences that are too broad. It is certainly the case that *Teaser* does not subscribe to a fixed musical direction but it is all a matter of taste and this may not be a bad thing.

Evidently, throughout his work before his solo career, Bolin was capable of, and indeed very good at, writing and playing in a range of styles. *Teaser* being reflective of that only goes to show the diversity of interest that was emerging in Bolin's music through his solo career. Bolin's intent for embracing a range of genres on the *Teaser* album is apparent in July 1975 in *Sounds,* where he said:

> I'm going into the studio next week. Half will be Cobham style jazz, the other rock. There's gonna be some great singles. The rock part will be as rock as Deep Purple, but there'll be a lot like the *Spectrum* album.

Oh and the reviewer's comments on Tommy's vocals? Well, you'll have to hear them for yourself. The emotion and beauty of tone that Bolin's vocals portray on the tracks 'People, People' and 'Wild Dogs' certainly contradict the reviewer's criticism. In terms of range, Bolin doesn't particularly push himself vocally, but that could simply be symptomatic of a musician who recognises the importance of working realistically within his own technical scope and limitations. Bolin's ability to know his limitations vocally was evidenced in an interview with *The Drummer* in January 1976 where he said:

> I had all these tunes that were right for my album (*Teaser*), but they needed a more raucous-type voice. Some of them were too difficult for me to sing. So I presented them to the group (Deep Purple), and we did the ones they liked. David Coverdale wrote the lyrics for most of them.

The songwriting work that Bolin had already done while working on *Teaser* (and indeed previously) was very much to Deep Purple's advantage. Ever the

Above: A publicity photo of a relaxed Tommy Bolin.

Left: The striking cover for Zephyr's debut album from 1969. *(Probe)*

Right: The back cover of Zephyr's debut album (left to right); Robbie Chamberlin, David Givens, Candy Givens, John Faris, Tommy Bolin. *(Probe)*

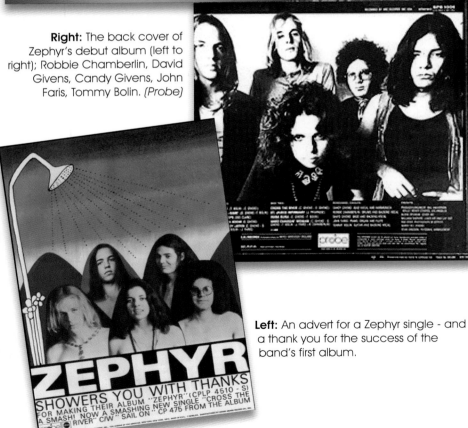

Left: An advert for a Zephyr single - and a thank you for the success of the band's first album.

Right: An advert for what looks like a double header between Zephyr and a band called Blues Image in 1970.

Left: An interesting line up for an event in 1970, with Zephyr second on the bill.

Left: James Gang's 1973 *Bang* album, Tommy's first with the band. *(Atco)*

Right: A rather more straightforward cover for the follow up to *Bang*, James Gang's *Miami* album from 1974. *(Atco)*

Left: A wanted poster! A James Gang concert poster from 1973.

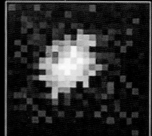

Right: Billy Cobham's 1973 *Spectrum* album, a landmark in many ways and a real showcase for Bolin's talents. *(Atlantic)*

Left: The Moxy album from 1975, featuring some somewhat understated cover art. *(Polydor)*

Right: Alphonse Mouzon's *Mind Transplant* album from 1975 which featured Bolin. It is a fusion masterpiece. *(Blue Note)*

Left: The cover of Deep Purple's *Come Taste The Band* album from 1975. *(Purple)*

Above: Deep Purple Mk IV, (left to right); David Coverdale, Ian Paice, Jon Lord, Tommy Bolin, Glenn Hughes.

Right: Promotional poster for the infamous Indonesian part of Deep Purple's 1976 tour in Jakarta.

Left: Tap dancing indeed! An advert for the band's early 1976 tour. Left to right: Ian Paice, Tommy Bolin, Jon Lord, David Coverdale, Glenn Hughes.

Right: To the beach! A poster for a Long beach show in February 1976.

Deep Purple

PLUS SPECIAL GUEST **Nazareth**

LONG BEACH ARENA
·300 EAST OCEAN BOULEVARD·
FRIDAY FEBRUARY 27th
TICKETS ON SALE NOW AT THE ARENA BOX OFFICE
RESERVED SEATS $6.50 $5.50 $4.50

deep purple

uk tour 76

Official Programme

Left: Deep Purple's UK 1976 tour programme.

Right: A ticket for a Deep Purple Florida show in 1976.

DEEP PURPLE

IN CONCERT

GENERAL ADMISSION

09610

FEB'RY **6** 1976

NO REFUNDS

Fri. Eve. at 8:00

Est. Pr. 5.76 | **TOTAL**

St. Tax .24 | **$6.00**

LAKELAND CIVIC CENTER

LAKELAND, FLORIDA

ITALY TASTE THE BAND

Thanks to the **DEEP PURPLE** *the Million Sellers! Ciao...*

EMI ITALIANA S.p.A.
Edizioni Musicali

Left: Deep Purple Mk IV had global success. This is an Italian press advert celebrating the sales of Deep Purple albums over the year.

Right: Das ist gut! The album also clearly did well in Germany.

DANKE SCHÖN DEEP PURPLE for letting us share your tremendous success

FRANCIS, DAY & HUNTER GMBH
2 HAMBURG 13, MITTELWEG 149 TEL.: 410 30 84

'DOWN UNDER'
EMI SALUTE DEEP PURPLE
FOR SALES IN EXCESS OF
A 2·5 MILLION

from
EMI
RECORDS & TAPES

2·5 MILLION

Left: Success in Australia! Another celebratory advert for the sales of Deep Purple albums.

We are happy, having been associated for so long with the talents of

UNIVERSAL SONGS

DEEP PURPLE
"You Keep On Moving!"

Amsterdam—25—Oranje Massaulaan
Brussels—2—Rue Jules Lebrun

Right: Well done, Deep Purple MkIV. This advert promotes concerts in Belgium and the Netherlands.

Thirsty?

DEEP PURPLE
Come taste the band

TPSA 7515
Also available on cassette and cartridge

Harvey Goldsmith presents
Deep Purple on tour:

March 11th Granby Hall – Leicester
March 12th EMPIRE POOL – LONDON
March 13th EMPIRE POOL – LONDON (sold out)
March 14th Apollo – Glasgow
March 15th Empire – Liverpool

Presented by Earley Associates

Appearing with special guests, a new Harvest Records signing, **STRAPPS**

Purple Records Ltd
Marketed by EMI Records Limited

Left: An advert for the *Come Taste The Band* tour and album in the UK in March 1976.

Right: Promotional material documenting a wealth of career success in support of the *Teaser* album in 1975.

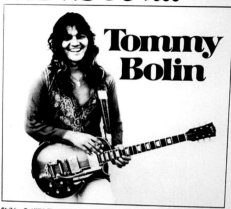

ALL ABOUT...

Tommy Bolin

Striking Out With The Kid From Sioux City...

... is leaving the fold and hitting the road on your own. **Tommy Bolin** has seen a lot of heavy-duty axe-action. He's been a veteran performer within some of the fastest moving bands in America.

First starting out in Denver's premier boogie band, **Zephyr**. Within a few short years, Tommy's growing legendary heat caught the ear of jazzman **Billy Cobham** who invited the kid from Sioux City to take part in the **Spectrum** sessions, where word-of-mouth carried his guitar doctrines faster than a speeding bullet.

The sessions paid off fast. Tommy landed a key position when **James Gang** leader **Joe Walsh** recommended him for admission. His esoteric musical beliefs contributed songs and lead axe riffs on two James Gang albums.

Then his brazen musical pulse quickened as he slipped into the hot shoes of Richie Blackmore in answer to **Deep Purple**'s plea for help, resulting in **Come Taste the Bang**, a skillfully tight mixture of searing arrangements and melody.

But the man needed to have a band to call his own when he agreed to go solo on Nemperor Records, resulting in **Teaser**, an album that did more than tickle his fans fancy.

At 25, **Tommy Bolin** comes to Columbia with a mind of his own and a conviction that his debut album is going to strike Gold.

PC/PCA 34329

Take a look into "Private Eyes." By Tommy Bolin.

There are
at things.
(especiall
music) is
Look the
reputatio
is hard to
dazzling
every ba
member of — from the James Gang
to Deep Purple.
Now. Look at "Private Eyes." PC 34329
Tommy Bolin's debut Columbia
recording features Mark Stein
(Vanilla Fudge) on keyboards and
Norma Jean Bell (Mothers of
Invention) on saxophone.
Together with Tommy, they make
a synthesis of metal and
jazz/soul that is fascinating.
**Tommy Bolin. His new album is
"Private Eyes."** Listen,
take a good, long look.
On Columbia Records and Tapes.

TOMMY BOLIN
PRIVATE EYES
including:
Post Toastee/Shake The Devil
Gypsy Soul/Sweet Burgundy
You Told Me That You Loved Me

Left: Promotional material for *Private Eyes* in 1976. *(Columbia)*

Left: The cover of *Teaser*, Tommy Bolin's first solo album from 1975. *(Nemperor)*

Right: The somewhat difficult to read back cover of the *Teaser* LP. *(Nemperor)*

If you missed Deep Purple's concert this week, after you've finished kicking yourself go out and buy Tommy Bolin's solo album

Teaser

K50208   Distributed by Atlantic

Left: Good advice to those that missed the Deep Purple shows.

Right: Deeply poignant. A ticket from Tommy Bolin's final performance on December 3, 1976.

LOGE

SEC	ROW	SEAT
F	14	1

ADMIT ONE   THIS DATE

DEC 3 1976

CELLAR DOOR CONCERTS PRESENTS
J E F F
B E C K
MIAMI
JAI-ALAI
DEC 3 1976
FRI 8 30 PM
6.25 + .25TAX

NO REFUNDS PRICE NO EXCHANGES

$6.50

SEC	ROW	SEAT
F	14	1

LOGE

KVAN
Presents

RUSH

with special guest **Tommy Bolin**

Saturday, October 30, 1976 — 11:30 p.m.

Paramount Theatre

$6.50 Day of Show   Get Down Productions

N° 034

Above: A ticket from a few weeks earlier, when Bolin supported Rush.

TOMORROW CLUB Presents

TOMMY BOLIN

- AND -

EARL SLICK

18 & Over — No Refunds

GENERAL

OCT.	SUNDAY EVENING Doors Open at 8:00 P.M.
3 1976	$3.00 (Advance) $4.00 (Day of Show)

Left: A ticket from a performance at the Tomorrow Club in October 1976.

Right: A poster advertising the 1994 Tommy Bolin convention in Sioux City, Iowa in 1994.

Left: *Tommy Bolin Captured Raw.* One of many posthumous releases, preserving a legacy of beautiful music.

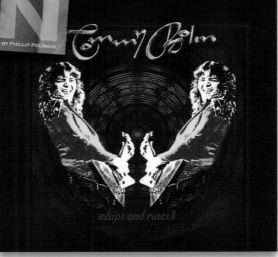

Right: Whips And Roses II from 2006. *(Steamhammer)*

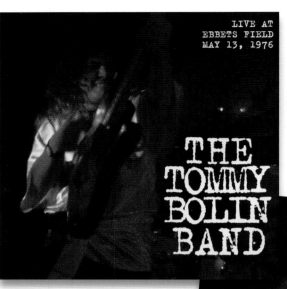

LIVE AT EBBETS FIELD MAY 13, 1976

THE TOMMY BOLIN BAND

Left: *Live At Ebbets Field.* A fantastic posthumous live release, featuring emotive and skilful musicianship. *(Tommy Bolin Archives)*

Right: *Live Archives 1976.* Another posthumous release full of stunning music. *(Breakdown, 2019)*

TOMMY BOLIN
BAND
Archives 1976
PARAMOUNT THEATRE, SEATTLE, WA 1976
TACOMA ARMORY, TACOMA, WA 1976

TOMMY BOLIN
LIVE IN NEW ORLEANS 1976

Left: *Live In New Orleans 1976,* released in 2019. Another fine example of Tommy Bolin in his element. *(Gypsy Eye Project)*

generous professional who seemed happy to share the spotlight, there are several interviews in which Tommy expressed an interest in working with more vocalists during the solo period of his career.

The diversity of musical styles that features on *Teaser* is valued positively in other reviews. The following is from the *Albuquerque Journal* on 18 January 1976:

Conceptually and musically, and even down to the title, it is a teaser, with an important difference: this first solo album by Tommy Bolin is completely accessible and satisfying… The biggest teaser is the range of the music is so tastefully written and performed by this heavy metal refugee, the same Tommy Bolin who jumped from the losing proposition of a Joe Walshless (sic) James Gang to fill the obnoxious shoes of Ritchie Blackmore when he departed (from) Deep Purple. Power rock is Bolin's base, but he proves himself equally adept at jazz, balladeering (sic), and even Latin rhythms. The overdubbing of several guitars on each number makes for rich textures throughout, and even within songs, you find him picking, strumming, sliding, leaping out front with wailing lead lines while maintaining understated electric and acoustic rhythms. Bolin's talented sidemen seem to have given him just what he wanted. David Foster's piano and synthesiser, respectively, in the first two songs, are as memorable and vital as the sizzling guitars. The second cut on each side is instrumental and jazz-based, particularly 'Marching Powder'… *Teaser* shows tremendous promise for Tommy Bolin as a solo performer. It's diverse enough to keep your attention through repeated listening, so solid that flaws never extend to the point of weakening an entire song. Though I like every cut, I can't let this review end without mentioning my favourite, the one that's getting the most airplay locally; 'Savannah Woman'. A nightclub cha-cha with seductive lyrics appropriately delivered, Bolin's lead, rhythm and fills are delightfully anachronous. This heavy but eclectic rocker may even have listened to Django Rheinhardt at some point.

Teaser was a sign of what Bolin was capable of. He was just getting started and this was advocated in a review of *Teaser* in March 1976 in *Circus*:

If *Come Taste the Band* follows the usual super-tight pop format of Deep Purple's previous English (loud) blooze (sic) material, *Teaser* aims for far wider realms, demonstrating that Tommy Bolin can not only rock hard and heavy, he can also fly. Released from the constraints of Purple's formula, Bolin literally lifts off from Mother Earth with an excellently recorded item sure to plug up any remaining holes you might have about him deserving Ritchie Blackmore's position in that band. On the strength of his own LP, we'd have to say he probably won't be with any group that does not bear his name for very long. When Tommy Bolin begins to come out of his shell, growing as his progress thus far indicates he surely can, we'll really have something to scream about. You can bet on it.

Even while with Deep Purple, Tommy had a world that existed away from the troubles of touring with them and *Teaser* is proof of that. Certainly, the Deep Purple tour was receiving more publicity than Tommy's *Teaser* album. Deep Purple had far more promotional force behind them (more money, higher profile, more stakeholders etc. etc.). In such regard, over forty years later, it is well worth giving *Teaser* a listen and appreciating it outside of all of the imbalances that seemingly went against Tommy at the time. The review of *Teaser* in December 1975 in *Billboard* certainly favours such perspective:

Guitarist Tommy Bolin goes full circle musically here. There's a little bit of everything on this LP, as Bolin plays some jazz, rock and even reggae. As a guitarist, he's one of the best around as evidenced by his work with Billy Cobham, James Gang and Deep Purple, and he gets a chance to shine on his own with this record. Into the last half of the seventies, Tommy Bolin is fast on his way to becoming a rock and roll legend. On his debut album, Bolin's guitar mastery, songwriting strength, and production prowess team up to make an eclectic album with mass appeal as well as artistic integrity. With the genres of rock, jazz, blues and Latin rhythms blended by Tommy's guitar and vocal work, *Teaser* boasts something for every radio programmer and record buyer. Through his early work with Billy Cobham and James Gang, now with his addition as the lead guitarist of Deep Purple and a brilliant debut album on Nemperer, Tommy Bolin is the vanguard of pop music's new leaders.

Chapter Seven: Private Eyes

Post-Deep Purple, it was time to move on. By March 1976 Tommy Bolin had already formed a band with whom to play live and work in the studio. Bolin recorded his second and final solo album after *Teaser, Private Eyes*. It was recorded in June 1976 at Cherokee Recording Studio in Los Angeles and mixed at Trident Recording Studios in London. It was released in September 1976 by Columbia. In an interview with *Billboard* in November 1976, Bolin said;

It's important having your record company behind you and Columbia is. The product is there I feel. Your album has to sell if the concerts are going to be successful. The audience has to know what it's listening to.

Private Eyes was to be Tommy's last studio album released while he was alive. In September 1976 in *The Drummer*, Tommy explained;

I was originally going to call the album (he doesn't specify which one, but it is likely to be *Private Eyes* based on the date of the interview) *Whips And Roses* because of the music, the whips being the hard stuff, and the roses being the soft mellow things. I thought it was nice, but everybody else thought it was stupid.

Tommy's idea for an album title was later honoured posthumously with the two *Whips And Roses* albums in 2006. They feature previously unreleased studio material of Tommy's. As with the *Teaser* album, Bolin's passion for a range of musical styles was fully present on the *Private Eyes* album. While some may accuse him of being stylistically inconsistent, I would advocate that this is a strong point of interest for both albums because it keeps the music interesting and it is fascinating to hear how versatile Tommy's abilities are both as a musician and as a writer. In the same interview, Tommy said;

It's (*Private Eyes*) different from the last, and I'd like every album to be different.

This was a musician who was not afraid to play across a range of styles. To be as experimental, as he was, is surely to be applauded. It was by this point in his career that Tommy had just started to come into his own. Having gone through the experiences of being viewed as the replacement for somebody else in both James Gang and Deep Purple, it seems that Bolin had reached the point of musically, knowing what he wanted and how he was going to go about it. In his same interview with *The Drummer*, he said;

No, I won't be joining any other bands. I'm gonna concentrate on my own. The Purple thing was great for a while, but it started to get a little too tense. I'm still great friends with them, it was more a management problem. They were hassling me with this and that... money wise it got kind of weird me being an American and them being English, so I just quietly removed myself. I'm sick of diving in other people's pools. Ian (Paice) and Jon (Lord) are working on albums, and Glenn Hughes has a double album coming out. He says he wants to put together a soul band or something like that. He's got the pipes for it; a real incredible singer. David Coverdale's album should be out by now. I'm as interested as anyone to see what they can do. I thought the album we did together (***Come Taste The Band***) was a good album. I guess Purple freaks were used to hearing the same thing they had always heard before.

It is apparent that by the time Bolin started working on his *Private Eyes* album in 1976, he was at the beginning of an exciting new direction both musically and personally. He was finally starting to take control of things; he was no longer in a situation where he was being criticised for the way in which he did or did not fill another musician's shoes. For the creation of the *Private Eyes* album, Bolin had reached a point where he was able to reject the needs and motives of other people. As Peter Crescenti wrote in the July 1976 issue of *Sounds*:

What I saw when I accompanied the band (Deep Purple) on their Japanese tour last December was a group of really talented but terribly frustrated musicians who had shackled themselves to an image, even though they were capable of creating a new identity, and probably a fantastic band, with a balls-up-front effort to communicate their new music. Instead, they plodded on, pretending to believe it but in reality, compromising themselves every time they walked on stage.

Crescenti's assessment of the situation seems very fair and I would suggest that it is such thing that makes Tommy's *Private Eyes* album so great; it is symptomatic of the fact that he was now free from having to contend with the dramas of an established band. Bolin was now in a position where he could really create something without all of the politics that came with his experiences in Deep Purple, both within the band and amongst the fans. It comes across that in terms of his career at least, during the days of making the *Private Eyes* album, Tommy was in a good place. As he wrote on the cover notes of the album: 'Extra special love and thanks to the most wonderful band I've ever had the pleasure to work with'. In September 1976 in *The Drummer*,

Bolin spoke enthusiastically both of the band who played on *Private Eyes* and those who would be touring with him:

Most of the people that were on the sessions with me are in the band now. Norma Jean Bell is in the band playing sax and on vocals. I met her through Michael Walden of Mahavishnu who was my original drummer, and she's just a real gas to play with. It's the same with bass guitarist Reggie McBride, who's been with The Stylistics and The Dramatics, and Stevie Wonder. Mark Stein is also in the band on keyboards. He's one of the original Vanilla Fudge, with Carmine Appice and Tim Bogert. Carmine's even on one track ('Someday Will Bring Our Love Home') because the drummer that was on the session nodded out. Like with all these people, doing the album was great.

In November 1976 in *Billboard*, Bolin explained:

I left Deep Purple to do my own album. Most of my musical growth was reflected in the bands I played in. I needed room to grow. Things are more comfortable now. I can get away with playing different types of music. I feel my music is more mature and I know what crowds want to hear. My main problem in the past was management. Barry (Fey)'s been a friend for seven years, managing me on and off. I'm happy with the way everything is now going.

As was reported in November 1977 in *Billboard*:

The first act handled by Feyline (Fey's company) was the late Tommy Bolin. According to industry insiders, Barry did more than a laudable job with him. When distribution of Bolin's records was too slow to suit Fey, he personally supervised speedier delivery of the albums at his own expense.

Tommy Bolin produced *Private Eyes* with Dennis Mackay who he had met at Trident Studios in London in 1975 while working on *Teaser*. Mackay is credited as the producer on some of the tracks on *Teaser*; 'People, People' and 'Marching Powder'. *Private Eyes* is a more cohesive album than *Teaser* as it is performed by one band rather than a variety of personnel on each track. Bobby Berge, who had worked with Tommy in Zephyr, plays drums. It feels like the band are on the same page in terms of the mood of the album, and the playing is more mellow than the intense high-speed solos that Tommy played on Billy Cobham's *Spectrum* album. *Private Eyes* is certainly not a jazz fusion record, but the influences are certainly there in terms of everything that Tommy's career had been building towards. There is much syncopation and funk played at a chilled yet engaging tempo. Norma Jean Bell is great on

sax, and as with the *Teaser* album, *Private Eyes* is worth a listen purely on the basis of the saxophone parts alone. Once you hear them on the opening track, 'Bustin' Out For Rosey', there's a reasonable likelihood that you'll want to keep listening - that's what really got me into Tommy Bolin's work as a whole. Reggie McBride plays bass in a way that has elements of call and response to Bolin's guitar playing. With Bobbye Hall on percussion and Mark Stein on keyboards, *Private Eyes* features a band that consists of talented individuals who play well together. In the looser parts of the album where the band jam, each musician gave the others room to contribute in a way that did not try to overshadow anyone else. It's a great album and worth a listen, both in its own right and as a representation of Tommy Bolin at his best. Indeed, there seems to be quite a poignancy surrounding the *Private Eyes* album. It is reflective of what could have been, had Tommy Bolin lived longer but also, it is equally reflective of a musician who did not deserve the emotional pains that he perhaps experienced when touring with Deep Purple. In terms of audience respect, Tommy Bolin deserved better and so does his legacy. If you do nothing else after reading this book, I strongly urge you to listen to *Private Eyes*. In September 1976, *Billboard* suggested that on *Private Eyes*:

> (Bolin's) guitar work is beautifully imaginative and blended with saxophones and percussion for some of the finest funky and progressive rock and jazz-rock to come down the pike in some time.

Also, *Private Eyes* received a very encouraging review in September 1976 in *Cash Box*:

> In his first Columbia LP, Tommy Bolin turns in some expected hard-driving rock guitar and some unexpectedly fine vocals. Since his days with Deep Purple, Bolin has continued to expand his work to include other musical genres, and here he displays a serious interest in phrasing and tone. Many of the tunes are based around some complicated instrumental riffing, with interesting rhythmic counterpoint provided by solid bass work. 'Shake The Devil' and 'You Told Me That You Loved Me' should be immediately slated for progressive rock play, while 'Gypsy Soul' is a fully realised ballad with Spanish flavour.

I support this review as a good and accurate reflection of what *Private Eyes* is about as an album overall. The hard rock elements that were present in *Teaser* (and indeed *Come Taste The Band*) are present, but equally, many of the tracks substantiate the view that Tommy had the skills and creativity to make an album that features a range of other interesting styles and genres. On *Private*

Eyes, Tommy's vocals are engaging; he sings with conviction and style. It is possible that *Private Eyes* could have signified the beginning of Tommy being regarded as not just a guitarist, but as a vocalist. Tommy had recorded some solo demos of songs for *Private Eyes* and these demos were released in 2002 by the Tommy Bolin Archives on a CD titled *Naked Volume II*. What is notable about the demos on this release is that Tommy played all of the instruments on them, including bass and drums. This release certainly evidences Bolin's wider abilities as a musician and indeed as a songwriter who was able to bring his ideas into being independently. As Bolin said in the January 1976 issue of *The Drummer*:

> Learning to play all those instruments was a big help for me in learning how to feel and phrase things musically. Playing the drums also showed me how important rhythm sections are to the sound. For me, if it doesn't rock, it doesn't motivate. With that kind of background, I can really appreciate how great it is to play with Ian Paice and Glenn Hughes.

Once recording had finished for the *Private Eyes* album, the Tommy Bolin Band began touring. Although one band lineup completed the *Private Eyes* album, the tour lineup changed at various points - see the list at the end of this book for all specific personnel details. Recordings from some of the live shows were released posthumously. They are listed in the discography of this book and are worth a listen; they are demonstrative of some great live musicianship, both from Bolin and the rest of the band. In June 1976 in *Sounds*, Peter Crescenti reviewed one of Tommy's gigs at the time. The review drew on what Crescenti considered to be Bolin's difficulty with consistency in live performances. It is difficult to comment on this one because all performers have bad days and in such regard, Bolin may not have been unusual.

Was Bolin exceptional in the extent of his inconsistencies as a live performer? It's a very subjective thing. It is often suggested that during Bolin's time with Deep Purple, his best contributions happened in the studio rather than on stage. Equally though, it is suggested that during the Zephyr days, the studio environment felt alien to the band and they were happier and more at ease performing live. There are so many contextual factors to consider when deciding whether to subscribe to the viewpoint that Tommy Bolin was inconsistent as a live performer. The review does allude to the possibility that drugs may have been a factor in the quality of the performance. I hate to say it, but it certainly is a strong possibility. However, the musical legacy of Tommy Bolin should be celebrated and remembered for what it is: sensitive, clever, and inventive. While it is indeed worth noting that drugs may have impacted his performance at times, it's important not to let this hearsay define him.

Greater focus must always remain on the music.

Another point of interest from the review is that Crescenti commented positively on Bolin's ability to share the spotlight with other band members. This is indicative of a generous person both personally and professionally. Had he lived longer, this might have been a significant benefit to his future career. Poignantly, the review is titled, 'Unloved and Somewhat Slightly Dazed.'

Tommy Bolin's debut New York City gig at the Bottom Line had to be a disappointment for the guitarist and his musicians. A dreadfully apathetic crowd, who seemed to have no interest in Bolin at all, either slowly straggled out in twos and threes, or sat as if in stupor, one which just about matched Bolin's own. Tommy looked dazed and confused – dazed by who knows what, and confused, probably, by the cold crowd reaction. I can write this gig off in my own mind though because just two nights earlier I'd seen Bolin's band rip through a dynamite set out at My Father's Place, a Long Island club, packed with Bolin freaks. Night one, show one, at the Bottom Line though, had to be one of the month-long tour's least memorable performances. Bolin's group is definitely impressive, with Mark Stein, founder of New York's own Vanilla Fudge, on organ and mini-Moog, Michael Walden, the post-Cobham Mahavishnu Orchestra drummer, bassist Reggie McBride, and the superfine Norma Jean Bell on sax. Norma's done gigs with Stevie Wonder and Frank Zappa, and her playing throughout the Bolin set is some of the best rock sax you're likely to hear. Bolin's decision was not to run a guitar band, so he gives all his players a lot of space to roam, within the confines of each tune. Bolin's black rhythm section gives his *Teaser* material a funky edge it doesn't have on the album, with the title track especially benefiting from McBride's boogie runs. Norma Bell consistently serves up soulful, biting flurries on her horn, and when she and Bolin do a riff together, she never is intimidated by the overpowering raunch of his guitar. Her solo in Bolin's reggae rocker, 'People, People' was an absolute delight. Meanwhile, over on keyboards, Mark Stein is always smiling like a madman, waving his arms and jumping off his bench, very obviously enjoying his return to the stage. He sings harmonies with Bolin and Bell, does a long moody Hammond/Moog solo intro into 'The Dreamer' (sic) and later does a lead vocal in the soulful 'I Fell In Love', which was easily one of the few really intense moments of the set. At the end of the song, when Bolin asked for a hand for The Sniffettes, himself, Norma and Reggie on backup vocals, someone from the audience wanted to know if Bolin was tripping. Probably not, but he was leaning up against a column on the stage and Norma Bell a lot. Michael Walden did a lead vocal too, in his own 'Delightful', from a forthcoming solo LP. He did a drum solo too, but failed, where he succeeded Saturday night, to arouse the audience to join him in shouting some jungle chants. A segue into 'Lotus' finished the set, with Bolin ripping off his best shot for the night, literally tearing at his guitar, probably spurred by a combined sense of disappointment and frustration. Not even an encore, where two nights earlier the band did a sweaty five number encore which lasted almost as long as the regular set. At this stage in his solo career, Bolin's problem is consistency and giving himself the chance to develop into the kind of musician he flashes the potential for. His vocals are adequate and can be improved with some tutoring, but too often they are flat and toneless like he isn't paying very much attention to the song. His guitar playing is still fiery, but when Bolin isn't all there on stage, neither are all his chops, so not even his hot guitar was there to save the night.

In May 1976, *Cash Box* reviewed a live performance of Tommy's that took place at The Roxy in Los Angeles:

The live tunes seemed even better than on Bolin's LP, *Teaser*, and with the exception of drummer Michael Walden, none of the stage band performed on record. Bolin's band, which he referred to as family, is a total versatile group effort. Those most outstanding were keyboardist Mark Stein and saxophonist Norma Bell, whose backup vocals would have augmented the album considerably. Oddly enough, several people had come just to see how messed up Bolin would be and if he'd do an encore collision of falling off the stage. Well, he didn't. In fact, the dramatics were deleted from the performance completely. The band was so intuitive of each other's moves and the set so tight that the power of the music carried the show without any dramatics.

It is plausible that the 'falling over' might refer to the following occurrence, as was reported in January 1976 in *Record World*:

Deep Purple guitarist Tommy Bolin was almost a rock and roll casualty at the group's concert in Largo, Maryland last week when he slipped on a patch of ice created by the group's smoke machine and fell twelve feet off the stage. He was OK and returned for the group's encore.

It's great to consider that in the live gig at The Roxy, Tommy proved the doubters wrong. It's a real shame that there was an emphasis on him having to do this throughout his entire career.

Tommy Bolin's final live show was on 3 December 1976 when he opened for Jeff Beck. Bolin's set on the night included performances of his songs 'Teaser' and 'Wild Dogs'. In a painful twist of irony, the set also included his song 'Post Toastee' from the *Private Eyes* album. The song is about the dangers and losses of taking drugs. What a great song it is too, the studio version is a nine-minute long epic that showcases Bolin's talent beautifully and includes complex percussion, gorgeous vocal harmonies and diverse guitar soloing. Fans in attendance at the show had no idea that they were bearing witness to the final show of a rising star and that his life was to be cut so suddenly short straight after. Surrounded by cheers from the audience, when Tommy left the stage that night, it would be his last. Tragically, in an interview after the show with *The Miami News*, Tommy was quoted as having said:

> I've been taking care of myself my whole life. Don't worry about me. I'm going to be around for a long time.

Just hours later and six months after recording his *Private Eyes* album, Thomas Richard Bolin was found dead in his hotel room from a drug overdose on 4 December 1976. *The New York Times* reported on 7 December 1976:

> Mr Bolin, twenty-five years old former lead guitarist with the Deep Purple rock group, performed at the head of his own new band Friday night in a concert at the Miami Jai Alai Fronton. Friends said afterward Mr Bolin had returned to his hotel and had drunk heavily with other members of the band until 2 A.M. when he retired. An hour later, friends found him semiconscious on the floor of his bathroom and put him back in bed. At 7 am, he was found dead.

He was just twenty-five. So much talent. So much potential. Cut so tragically short. A young prodigy who had more to give. Painfully, the world can only wonder about what could have been.

Left and below Two adverts for back to back solo headliner shows in California in late April and early May 1976.

Left: A magazine listing for a triple bill in July 1976, featuring Santana and Moxy as well as Tommy's band.

Below A somewhat poignant poster for 12 December 1976, when Tommy was due to open for Jeff Beck. Sadly, Tommy died just eight days before the show was due to take place.

Chapter Eight: His Legacy Lives On

Tommy Bolin was an artist of remarkable talent. He was a musical chameleon, able to change his playing and writing to suit the demands of a whole range of situations and requirements. His playing covered many musical styles including hard rock and jazz fusion. While he was stylistically diverse, he had a distinctive sound. He was self-taught, passionate, very much his own person and adept at conveying strong emotions in his music both vocally and with his guitar. Bolin had it all, talent, charm and looks. He never quite achieved superstar status but it is plausible that he could certainly have been on his way there having made two well-received solo albums. Sadly, we will never know. One thing is certain though, Tommy Bolin's music stands up in its own right and testament to this has been the enthusiasm from the people who seek to keep his legacy alive. Many of his recordings have been released posthumously by the Tommy Bolin Archives and a convention is held in Sioux City every year in his memory. From a young age, Tommy lived a nomadic existence. He was an interesting personality and was beginning to carve his own path both professionally and personally, despite the pains of the drug addiction that often overshadows his legacy due to its role in his demise. Bolin had so much potential and so much more to give to the world musically. His death at a young age was such that it is easy to argue that, as with many musicians who die young, his potential is romanticised based on what could have been. It feels vital to tell people to look beyond the bad press from the extreme highs and lows of Tommy's days in Deep Purple. Enjoy *Come Taste The Band* as a good studio album in its own right and further to this, embrace the fascinating and beautiful back catalogue that is Tommy Bolin's music outside of when he joined what would come to be known as Deep Purple Mk4 in 1975.

It comes down to this; no matter who was tasked with filling Blackmore's shoes, it was going to be an impossible job. Ritchie Blackmore is Ritchie Blackmore. There is nobody else like him, and his trademark music and stage presence brought the aggression, power and excitement into Deep Purple, particularly in their live performances. Although this is Tommy Bolin's story, it feels necessary to repeat that replacing Blackmore in Deep Purple would have been an uphill struggle for anyone in a situation where fans were aggrieved that Blackmore was no longer in the band. The hostility towards Tommy Bolin both musically and personally from some Deep Purple fans is something that would have probably been directed at anyone who was recruited to fill in for Blackmore after Deep Purple Mk3. As Geoff Barton eloquently put it in *Classic Rock* in February 2015:

The only problem with Blackmore's replacement? He wasn't Blackmore.

In August 2017 in *Classic Rock*, Barton quoted David Coverdale from a previous interview as having said:

When it was official that Ritchie was out, I immediately wanted to make a solo album – and the players I knew I wanted to work on it with me were the rest of Purple. My disappointment was in not changing the band name. I remember the meeting with the remaining band members and management following Ritchie's announcement. I suggested we call ourselves Good Company, Purple or The Deeps. I believed, and still do believe, that without Blackmore – his quirky character, personality, inspiration and influence – it couldn't be Purple. Ritchie was the creative driving force of the band. Of course, I was shot down in flames. Ultimately it was a business decision to continue as Deep Purple.

In the same article, Barton quoted Jon Lord posthumously:

I don't think it's (***Come Taste The Band***) a Purple record at all. I have to say that I took very little interest at the time in anything to do with the creative process. Had it not been for David and Glenn and Tommy in particular, I don't think the album would've got made. Glenn, in his lucid moments, was a powerhouse. Tommy seemed to thrive on being stoned. A lot of the groove and the drama were down to Tommy. Occasionally something fired me up. 'You Keep On Moving' is one of the great Purple tracks and a couple of others I find exceptionally good. I listened to the album recently and it's fabulous, it's one of the really great 1970s rock albums. But to me, it's not a Purple album. It's not a Purple album.

Ah, the power of hindsight! In July 1975 in *Sounds*, Lord had said:

I had a meeting with the band where I suggested that if we were going to stay together, we should change the name. The others said 'why? It'll be four members of Deep Purple plus another guitarist. If we call ourselves Larry The Lamb etc. it'll still be Deep Purple so why not keep the name?' I couldn't argue with that.

It is fascinating to consider that something as subtle and yet fundamental as a name change could perhaps have saved a lot of pain and frustration for everyone in the Mk4 lineup of Deep Purple, including Tommy. If Coverdale, Hughes, Lord, Paice and indeed Bolin were not under the banner of the Deep Purple brand, it could have helped to inform audience expectations and thus taken a lot of pressure off of everyone involved. Just one thing! A name change! It's incredible to think that this could have inspired an incredibly different

outcome for all concerned. This is especially the case in terms of how, as Glenn Hughes asserted:

I'm not sure if it was my 'funky shoeshine music' (Blackmore's infamous description of Purple's direction at that time) that was the last straw. Was it my fault that Ritchie left Deep Purple? Absolutely not. Let me make this clear; Coverdale and I were listening to the same kind of music in 1974. I'd go into his hotel room and he'd be playing Steely Dan, Marvin Gaye, Kool And The Gang, anything to do with black music. It wasn't just me. Even Paicey (Ian Paice) was doing it. Purple weren't a – quote, unquote – heavy metal band who had to follow a formula. We were evolving. But Ritchie wanted to go and play his Bach-infused music, which was one hundred miles from where I was going.

Deep Purple were knowingly taking their music in a drastically different direction before the Mk4 lineup, which, ironically, was considered to be a key reason for Blackmore's departure from Deep Purple. Before Bolin's involvement with the band, the Mk3 *Stormbringer* album in 1974 was such a shift in musical style that even Deep Purple's record company were surprised with it when first presented with the material. *Stormbringer* features a lot of funk and soul influences that are worlds away from the hard rock that was predominantly a trademark sound for the band, and indeed Blackmore. As a result of this, the remaining members of Deep Purple were not at all surprised when the *Stormbringer* album was a key catalyst for Blackmore deciding to leave the band in 1975. In August 1975 in *New Musical Express,* Coverdale said:

Ritchie was worried about the direction he thought the band might be headed in. He didn't like the soul that was creeping into the band. See, what Ritchie regards as funk are things like 'Sail Away' and 'Mistreated' and that's the direction the rest of us saw the band headed in.

The funk and soul influences that Glenn Hughes and David Coverdale added to Deep Purple were already in place on the *Stormbringer* album – and to some extent before that, the *Burn* album in 1974 - and thus, the stylistic interests of the band were already in place before Tommy Bolin was even considered for the new lineup. As was advocated in an article on funk-rock in December 2003 in *Classic Rock*:

Deep Purple, of course, took a more direct route to da funk (sic). Like all their contemporaries, their deep blues influences were in evidence from their earliest recordings, but speeded up, often as not, and eventually hung in the ornate classical frames keyboardist Jon Lord had begun to favour from the early seventies. That all changed, however, when first David Coverdale, then Glenn Hughes and finally, Tommy Bolin arrived and took the band in a whole new direction, probably best described as fusion rock: funky, jazzy, bluesy, rocky, with just enough old Purple signature flourishes to make it all work. As a result, *Come Taste The Band*, the only Bolin era Purple album was one of the bravest, most musically adventurous albums the band ever made; the one where they completely abandoned the tried and tested Purple formula and actually attempted something new.

It's not like Tommy came along and forced a change in the band that other members were not open to. Very much the opposite in fact; in August 2017 in *Classic Rock*, Barton quoted Coverdale:

No one had heard of Tommy, so I played them some bits of (Billy Cobham's) *Spectrum* and collectively they gave the thumbs up. Our US office was contacted to track Tommy down. We eventually found him living down the road from me in Malibu.

Clearly, after Blackmore left Deep Purple, the remaining band members already had an interest in soul, funk and jazz sometime before Tommy Bolin came to be an influence on their musical output. It seems that with hindsight, the members of Deep Purple who worked with Bolin have been keen to advocate as to why the Mk4 lineup struggled in the way that it did. Commercially, it was clearly a turbulent time. The album was relatively successful - it got to number 19 in the UK and to number 43 in the *Billboard* chart as well as being certified Silver on 1 November 1975 by the British Phonographic Industry. It had sold 60,000 copies in the UK by that point. However, during the live shows, audience behaviour towards Bolin certainly sounds like it was often much less than kind. It really is a shame because musically, as Coverdale said of *Come Taste The Band*:

I liked the album when it was new, to be honest. I felt as I do now, that it has some great moments.

In some cases, the media had decided that they didn't like Bolin and his recruitment into Deep Purple before they had even heard his musical contribution to the band. In August 1975, the *New Musical Express* portrayed Bolin in a particularly derogatory way:

Now Bolin's the new boy with just three weeks of Purple membership behind him. A month ago the former James Gang/Billy Cobham axeman was sitting on his butt searching out a gig. Today he's in the hot seat, having taken over the spot vacated by Purple's founder, that doomy, dark and moody king of heavy metal guitar, Ritchie Blackmore. After a couple of hours drinking and enjoying the more exotic fruits of rock 'n' roll success, the mood is hardly conducive to serious conversation, but we try. Seems that Coverdale and I will make it, but Bolin is a little further out into the cosmos... At the mention of his own name and getting stoned Bolin comes to life, brushing his peacock hair from his dilated pupils. The former replacement for Joe Walsh in the James Gang, then guest guitarist on Billy Cobham's excellent *Spectrum*, Bolin tried to speak; 'Uh... I'd been up all night... like... and I... er... wanted to call it off... but when we started playing...'.

Evidently, the article is burning with inaccuracy insinuating that Bolin was waiting around and doing absolutely nothing before being invited to audition for Deep Purple. That isn't true. Bolin was working on *Teaser*! The way the article in the *New Musical Express* was written could have easily led people to believe that Bolin was at a loose end and in desperate need of the Deep Purple opportunity. Speaking objectively in view of Bolin's career up to that point, that simply can't be true. Also, the article seems to go above and beyond to emphasise that Bolin presented for the interview in an inebriated state. While that could well have been true, was this really necessary in the name of good journalism, particularly where the journalist had failed to get some key facts right regarding Bolin's career prior to Deep Purple. I find this article in the *New Musical Express* particularly problematic because it backs up my assertion that Tommy Bolin wasn't even given a chance to be welcomed by Deep Purple fans with the negative publicity projected onto him by the media before Mk4 had even finished working in the studio.

It would seem that the *NME* just weren't particularly keen on Bolin full stop. In December 1975, their review of his *Teaser* album certainly comes across in such way. It seems to read like a school report with a 'could do better' through-line from a teacher who just doesn't like a particular student:

It's of little surprise to learn that Tommy Bolin is as much a rock 'n' roller in solo as he indicated that he is in a group situation on Deep Purple's *Come Taste The Band*. Some may find this disappointing, as there's obviously a considerable breadth and depth in his guitar style, which generally doesn't find expression through the more blatant rock frameworks. For instance, 'Dreamer' comes fairly close to presenting Bolin as an astute player of considerable discipline. Although eventually the track, with a piano that gives it a feel not unlike some of Bowie 'Honky Dory', hots up and opens out. This is though, a peculiarity of Bolin's music. There seems to be little middle ground – with the possible exception of 'Savannah Woman' – as he prefers to go straight from rather light melodies to dark, doom-laden power chords in one step. By the time you reach the final cut of the set, 'Lotus', you can successfully predict what sort of arrangement he'll choose. Bolin, with a cut like 'Marching Powder', does attempt to move into other areas of music, in this instance jazz improvisation, but not too successfully. Once again the volume whoops up and the rhythm section piles in unhesitantly (sic). Forget about taste, they're gonna have a blow. Bolin's view is obviously then very narrow, but as most of the compositions (eight of the nine tracks he either wrote or co-wrote) are merely vehicles for his own talents – either as guitarist or vocalist – there is a lot of good in the set. And he sounds like he enjoyed making the set.

In February 1991 in *Guitar World*, Mordechai Kleidermacher quoted Ritchie Blackmore talking about Bolin:

When I heard that Purple hired him, I thought he was great. He was always so humble. I remember he would always invite me out to his house in Hollywood to see his guitar. One day I went to his place. I walked in and tried to find him, but no one was around. There was no furnishings, nothing. I stayed there for ten minutes before he finally appeared. He showed me his guitar, and the strings must have had a quarter-inch of grime on them, as though he hadn't changed them in four years. I asked him when was the last time he'd changed the strings and he said very seriously, 'Gee, I don't know. Do you think I should change them?'

All I'll say on this is listen to Bolin's solo on 'Moon Rider' on the Moxy album. Listen to his solo work on Billy Cobham's *Spectrum* album. Listen to 'Alexis' on the *Bang* album by James Gang. Tommy certainly does not sound like a musician who was not in command of his guitar. In the same interview with Kleidermacher, Blackmore continued:

I originally heard Bolin on Billy Cobham's ***Spectrum*** album and thought 'Who is this guy?' Then I saw him on television and he looked incredible – like Elvis Presley. I knew he was gonna be big.

Blackmore's positive and empathetic approach towards Bolin also featured in *Guitar World* in May 1999 where Chris Gill quoted Blackmore as having said:

I don't envy Tommy Bolin trying to take my place in Purple. He was a uniquely talented player and it's unfortunate that he never had the chance to develop with the band the way that I did. His death was an incredible loss, not only for Deep Purple but for guitar fans as well.

To put it bluntly, Blackmore said it best here. Nothing about his comment on Bolin is anything to be disagreed with, not because he's Ritchie Blackmore and he's a genius – he is – but because Blackmore touches on what the main challenges were for Bolin as well as acknowledging how tragic it is that Bolin never quite got to fulfil the entirety of his potential, both with Deep Purple and due to his life being cut so devastatingly short. In August 1974 in *Guitar*, Blackmore discussed his own musical education:

It (classical music) was good training. It made me play properly, use all the fingers and not just the usual blues thing which is to use two or three fingers and copy records.

Also, in September 1975 in *Circus*, Blackmore advocated for the advantages of classical training, at least in the formative stages of a musician's career:

It (classical guitar lessons) got a bit tedious and I wanted to play rock, and I couldn't keep up with the classical playing, it was a bit stiff and I played everything by ear. I think it's very important when you first learn an instrument to go straight into the training of it to get things right because once you start picking up bad habits, you'll be stuck with them forever. It's like driving, you must learn properly from the beginning and then adapt to your own style. I learned to use all my fingers, while most blues guitarists only use three. I developed a name for playing very fast runs, but to me it wasn't fast, it's just that I've learned to use my little finger.

Blackmore's background of classical music training appears to be something that he valued as a foundation upon which to build for his writing and playing. He is often held in high regard for his use of Bach inspired chord progressions on tracks such as 'Highway Star' from Deep Purple's 1972 *Machine Head* album and the title track 'Burn' on Deep Purple's 1974 album. It is prominent that Deep Purple's fans had come to expect a particular brand of music by the time Tommy Bolin came to be involved with the band. In February 1976, *Billboard* compared Bolin's playing to Blackmore's from one of the Mk4 concert dates at Radio City Music Hall in New York:

Purple shied away from some of its best known single hits, 'Smoke On The Water' being its only concession to older material. The song, so often heard in its original form, really showed the stylistic changes made by the band's new vocal-guitar team. Bolin avoided the huge throbbing chord sequences that marked Ritchie Blackmore's style in favour of a more fragile, delicate approach. Consequently, the song lost some of its bite and Bolin acquitted himself better on his own compositions.

Bolin's differing approach to music theory was mentioned in October 1975 in *Electric Guitars,* where he spoke candidly:

I only ever had four lessons, but they wanted to teach me Hawaiian steel guitar for some reason and I wanted to play rock. I read some article which said I was a jazz guitar player. But I don't know any scales at all. So I don't really know what I'm doing. I know what to play, but don't know any scales because I never bothered to learn any. I would love to be able to read (sheet music), on the other hand, I wouldn't want to. You see people that can read and still have enough flexibility and sensitivity, and I'd like to be like that. When I was playing with Billy Cobham, there was a tune that I didn't know what key it was in, and I was too embarrassed to ask. And they gave me a chart, and I told them 'that just looks like a drawing to me'. So Jan Hammer taught me the theme and I did the lead parts. Jan is a great example of somebody who can read unbelievably well and can just go in and hear something and play it. Whereas I know a lot of great readers who can read as well as him, but when you sit down to play with them they have no feeling. I must admit, I don't know a lot of chords myself, I usually make them up. I've been playing a lot with Larry Coryell (an American jazz guitarist who was a key figure in the jazz fusion scene) and he's been teaching me. He spends hours, but I just can't learn it and usually end making it up.

Let's face it, Bolin was playing music for the purposes of performing rather than for preparing to pass music examinations and go to a conservatoire. This is the same with Blackmore really in a way. In many interviews, he stated that he didn't enjoy doing *Concerto For Group And Orchestra* and that he doesn't follow a score when playing. All of that was more of a Jon Lord thing. Classical training didn't inspire Bolin but having taken a different path into music didn't seem to hold him back either. It is definitely a case of, upon listening to his discography, judge him by his results rather than his methods. If someone can write songs like 'Bustin' Out For Rosey' and 'Alexis' without a formal grounding in music theory then more power to them.

 There is another aspect of his playing that separates Tommy Bolin from Ritchie Blackmore; Bolin excelled in the world of jazz fusion in his work with both Billy Cobham and Alphonse Mouzon. His playing on their *Spectrum* and *Mind Transplant* albums respectively was highly regarded to the extent that

it brought Bolin to the attention of other musicians. Indeed, so much so that his work on *Spectrum* was the thing that initially brought him to the attention of Deep Purple. Bolin excelled in an area of music that was unlikely to be of interest to Ritchie Blackmore. Blackmore spelt out his own lack of interest in jazz in August 1974 in *Guitar*:

> In jazz, you have a very broad construction. You can hit ninths, fifths, flattened ninths; things like that. In rock, you're limited, and that's the challenge. This might sound silly, but I feel jazz is too free. You can be playing with a jazzer and be up, and down that fingerboard and you can hit any note you want, it's going to work out a flattened ninth, a tenth, a thirteenth – it's going to be something. Even in a different key, it'll fit somewhere; I've done it. Take a progression like A, F sharp, D, and E, and they're experimenting and hitting diminisheds and augmenteds, so when they hit that A, you can play any note you like and it'll either be a flattened third, a flattened fifth, an added sixth or a suspended ninth. They can get away with murder, some of those guys. Great runs and things but because there's so much going on in the background it's bound to be related somewhere along the line, so it always fits. This is probably what they get off on. Whereas in rock, you can't. If somebody's hitting an A, you've got to stick around that A somehow.

It is vital to make it clear that Blackmore's comments on jazz were not made with regards to Bolin or any of Bolin's work. Bolin is not mentioned in that interview and it is possible that Blackmore was not even aware of Bolin or his work at the time. The point I am making is this; the musical interests and musical backgrounds of Blackmore and Bolin were so substantially different that it really does add weight to the argument that the band that came to be known as Deep Purple Mk4 really might have fared better under a different name entirely. Ritchie Blackmore made Deep Purple what it was in terms of classical music influences, riffs and hard rock. It just doesn't seem fair on Bolin to have asked him to fill the shoes of someone who was so different to him musically. Bolin was a talent in his own right. On the one hand, it feels like a risk to compare Bolin with Blackmore so explicitly as in, a key philosophy behind this book is to advocate for the fact that Bolin and Blackmore are two very different musicians so why should we compare them in the first place? However, the differences between both musicians and their approaches to making music are understandably a relevant factor in terms of how they both presented to audiences so differently. Again, it would be inappropriate to attempt to elevate the status of one musician above the other based on their educational background; at the end of the day they have both played extremely well throughout their careers. It's fascinating to think that perhaps Bolin wouldn't have been so drastically compared to Blackmore (if at all) if Lord, Paice, Hughes and Coverdale had just elected to name the band something other than Deep Purple when Bolin joined. Besides, the band that came to be known as Deep Purple Mk4 only had two of the band's original founding members by that point - Jon Lord and Ian Paice.

Tommy Bolin's background as a musician was clearly very different to that of Ritchie Blackmore's. There really is nothing problematic about that though. As a musician, Tommy was versatile and intuitive. He was a complete guitarist in that his talents went beyond the focus on playing lead. There was more to his rhythm playing than relying on standard bar chords. Of course, he did use standard bar chords because they are a staple element of hard rock, but it is evident that he was capable of so much more, as was the case across the scope of his career prior to Deep Purple. It is particularly apparent in both Billy Cobham's *Spectrum* album and Alphonse Mouzon's *Mind Transplant* that Tommy Bolin knew his funk chords and was capable of applying them brilliantly in the context of an ensemble piece. Although in several interviews, Bolin advocated that he had a minimal understanding of scales, he played a range of melodies that seem to be quite closely related to not only the minor pentatonic scale (that black piano note thing that I mentioned earlier) but in other instances, the Dorian and Aeolian scale – both of which can make melodies sound sentimental. When used in riffs, the pentatonic scale can make them sound oriental, an example of this is the riff to 'Love Child' on *Come Taste The Band*. The minor pentatonic scale features in a lot of Blackmore era Deep Purple song riffs too, for instance 'Speed King' (1970), 'Black Night' (1970) and 'Strange Kind Of Woman' (1971). Now, I'm not saying that someone can immediately be regarded as a good musician on the basis of whether or not they play in a way that can be related to patterns from established music theory. That would be specious reasoning and quite elitist in favour of just one approach to music. Whether the music theory approach to what Bolin was playing resonates or not, sit back, close your eyes and listen to his music. The man knew what he was doing and he did it well. Bolin's guitar picking style was often staccato with very fast phrasing. It doesn't always sound particularly disciplined in terms of technique but does it really need to? Tommy's solos feel more improvisational than worked out and this doesn't seem to be a bad thing at all; they were played with style and feeling in a way that was in the context of what the other musicians in any given ensemble were playing. Although Bolin stated in a number of interviews that he had no interest in scales, chords and generally embracing music theory from a heavily disciplined perspective, it is apparent in his playing that he certainly had a strong feel for the music. There was nothing in his playing to suggest such a lack of theoretical background. Such is the nature of having a good ear for music, perhaps.

It is imperative to discuss the live performances during the Japan part of the Deep Purple Mk4 tour. The reason for this is that all too often, many people perhaps subscribe to a narrative that seems to go something like this:

> Bolin incurred an arm injury from something to do with his drug habit and as a result, every live performance in Japan was awful and it was all Tommy's fault.

This is not true at all. I feel it is vital to really give the live stuff a good listen and to consider it objectively. Of course, there will be many Deep Purple fans out there who have already done this and still hold a negative opinion of Bolin's performance. Fair enough. But for fans who haven't given the live performances from Japan a good listen, I strongly urge you to do so. The more I have listened to Bolin's music over the years, the more positive my opinion of it has become. I'm glad I did this rather than subscribing to the feeling that seems to be shared among many Deep Purple fans. I could have missed out on some great music.

Anyway, Deep Purple Mk4 played their final live date in Japan on 15 December 1975 at the Budokan in Tokyo. The performance was recorded officially but also, as was not unusual at the time, unofficially by members of the audience as well. Apparently, the first bootleg of such recording was released on vinyl under the name *Get It While It Tastes*. I am stating this cautiously because such is the nature of the bootleg industry; they are often not catalogued. Of course, the official recoding that represented Deep Purple's performance in Japan at the time was the one that was released in March 1977 under the title, *Last Concert In Japan*. It was heavily edited and didn't do too well in reviews. In July 1978, the German magazine, *Rocky* stated that 'Der sound könnte besser sein' (it could sound better); 'Die Live-Atmosphäre kommt ganz gut rüber' (the live atmosphere comes across very well) but 'die nicht besonders inspirierten Deep Purple merklich an' (it's noticeable that Deep Purple are not particularly inspired). In an interview for the 1995 BBC documentary, *Rock Family Trees* (produced by Francis Hanly) Glenn Hughes asserted that the *Last Concert In Japan* album should never have been released on the basis that it was not a fair reflection of what the band was capable of. As a result, the *This Time Around – Live In Tokyo* album released in 2001 is arguably the best choice of album to listen to in order to get the most frank account of what Deep Purple Mk4 really sounded like live; it is essentially an official release of the same material that was on the bootleg, *Get It While It Tastes*.

The majority of material from the full live concert that features on *This Time Around – Live in Tokyo* is from the *Come Taste The Band* album. Although the tour in question was promoting that Mk4 studio album, this could be considered a bold move due to the fact that by this time in Deep Purple's history, fans may have had particular expectations to hear a lot of the band's classic and much-loved material that was written in the Blackmore era. That said, the concert opens with 'Burn' and to hear Bolin's contribution to this song is fascinating. In the interests of being objective about this, I'm not quite sure how to describe Tommy's playing of the infamous riff as the song gets going. I'm going to be honest, I would argue that it sounds quite sloppy. It is not as rhythmically tight as when Blackmore played it live (or indeed on the studio version). Every repetition of the riff sounds a bit different when Tommy plays it. As a listener, I can totally understand why many people would feel frustrated and think 'just play the riff!'. Discussing one of Deep Purple's earlier shows on the tour, Jon Lord advocated in March 1976 in *Circus*:

> It came off all right, but there was this mad whispering running across the stage, 'What the hell's next? How does that go?' We opened with 'Burn' and we were just going onstage. The lights go down and the audience is applauding, and Tommy says 'How the f*** does that riff go?'.

However, all that said, it is after playing the solo section of the song that Bolin goes back into playing the famous riff and post solo he seems to be playing the riff with more certainty, rhythm and power. Now then, Tommy's solo on this live performance of 'Burn' is something that strongly exemplifies how differently he approached the song compared to Blackmore; on the studio version and live, Blackmore often used a lot of techniques that are a staple part of his musical style. For instance, bars that are very Bach inspired and consist of mirrored patterns of many sixteenth and eighth notes. The same features are apparent in his 'Highway Star' solo from the 1972 *Machine Head* album and even as far on as where he quotes a section from Bach's *Toccata And Fugue* on the song 'Death Alley Driver' on the 1982 Rainbow album, *Straight Between The Eyes*. With Blackmore, the Bach influence was never far removed from his work.

Rhythmically, there is a lot more syncopation in Bolin's solo on 'Burn'. It is in such instances that his background, as someone who has played a lot of jazz, becomes prominent. It is a great solo. It is a solo that shows what Bolin sounds like at his best. If that's what he sounds like with an arm injury then wow! That's talent. Bolin's solo is full of flair and passion and it is reflective of someone who has a good mastery of the guitar and is adding something worthwhile to the context of the song overall. It is plausible that Bolin's solo in this performance of 'Burn' was the vehicle through which he gained the momentum that resulted in him going back into the riff section of the song in a way that does the original riff more justice. Aside from his excellent solo in 'Burn' that seems to get Bolin's playing up and running for the rest of the concert, his writing talents make a significant contribution to the live set, not only as a result of his credits on seven of the nine songs on the *Come Taste The Band* album but because he brings in some of his material from *Teaser*. It is fantastic to hear Deep Purple play 'Wild Dogs'. Firstly, because it is interesting to see what the band does with the song, but also because Glenn Hughes contributes backing vocals that add a lot of dimension in terms of texture and harmony. I advocate that this is a real treat for both Deep Purple and Bolin fans because it is the ultimate collaboration between Bolin as an artist in his own right and the talents of Deep Purple as an ensemble. There are of course a number of moments where Bolin's playing falters and sounds sloppy or perhaps even takes a while to get going. There is no way of telling if that's down to nerves or his infamous arm injury. On balance, though, such moments are a drop in the ocean in proportion to what the concert sounds like as a whole. 'Love Child', for example, is played with speed, power and precision. Essentially, I would argue that his performance is engaging, worthwhile and certainly not to the detriment of Deep Purple at all.

It's worth considering the influence of bootlegs here. The unedited nature of them doesn't allow scope for alterations to portray the band at their best. Equally though, the lack of such editing on bootlegs often results in a product that represents the live performance as organically as possible for anyone who wasn't there. It could be that the *Get It While It Tastes* helped Tommy, as his contribution to Deep Purple's live set was not censored by a record label. Although by the time Tommy Bolin was in Deep Purple, Roger Glover (bassist with the Mk2 lineup) was well out of the picture, his perspective on what bootlegs mean for Deep Purple in terms of the band's overall history is of interest. In July 2011 in *Goldmine*, Glover remarked:

> I could never understand our success; I could never understand why so many people bought our records because they were so full of flaws! And then I started listening to bootlegs and to what we really were, and I came to reassess the whole thing. Listening to bootlegs from the early 1970s, I realised what a dangerous band we were, and how exciting it was not to know what was going to happen next. We walked a very thin line between chaos and order, and that was the magic, that was why people bought our records. I came from a pop band (Episode Six), and when you're a pop band, you learn the song, and you play it the same way every night. And now, there's this band veering off, and suddenly the solo's in E when it should be … 'hey, what's happening here?' That's the magic.

Bootlegging is one of the major reasons why people are able to enjoy Tommy Bolin's music today, particularly his work outside of Deep Purple. Passionate fans of Tommy's have worked hard to source recordings of his studio and live material so that it can be released to preserve his musical legacy. In October 1989 in *Westword*, Gil Asakawa wrote:

> Tommy Bolin left a legacy: his music. Local radio stations still play tracks from the records he made in the mid-seventies with the James Gang and Deep Purple, as well as his two solo albums, *Teaser* and *Private Eyes*. But much of Bolin's work has been hard to find or out-of-print altogether. Until now, that is. This week, Geffen Records will release *Tommy Bolin: The Ultimate*..., a multiple-disc retrospective. The collection is a collaboration between two hardcore Bolin fans who thought his contributions to contemporary music shouldn't be forgotten – a Montana musician named Will Dixon, a Bolin archivist working with the blessings of Tommy's family, and Tom Zutaut, a Geffen Records executive who supervised the project. The set spans Bolin's career, stretching as far back as Zephyr, the Boulder group that was Bolin's first brush with stardom.

It is necessary to remember that the article I have quoted from is from 1989, thirteen years after Tommy's passing. It documents what was to be just the beginning of building Tommy Bolin's musical legacy. Since then, there have been many more releases (as are listed in the discography of this book). As Tom Zutaut said in an interview on the 1989 documentary, *Tommy Bolin: The Ultimate* (directed by Michael Drumm):

> The fact that Tommy's records were just unavailable to the next generation compelled me to do this. This music shouldn't be lost. It should be available. To me, it's a crime when music gets lost, and I mean a lot of music does get lost. There are a lot of great records out of print.

Recordings of Tommy Bolin's work that have been released posthumously are vital resources in being able to make a case for the argument that there was so much more to Bolin than Deep Purple. For instance, while Tommy's initial playing of the 'Burn' riff sounds quite sloppy on the Deep Purple album, *This Time Around – Live In Tokyo*, it is certainly not reflective of Tommy at his best. For an example of such thing, the posthumously released *Tommy Bolin Live At Ebbets Field, June 3 And 4 1974* is well worth a listen. The live show begins with Tommy playing a track called 'You Know, You Know'. The riff is so tight; it is played with rhythmic accuracy and Tommy plays it with precision each time he repeats it. In terms of Tommy's ability to play a riff well, this recording represents every element of technical precision and clarity that was lacking when he played the 'Burn' riff in 1975 as it features on the *This Time*

Around – Live in Tokyo album. Considering what Tommy is clearly shown to be capable of in a number of his posthumously released recordings, I find this considerably frustrating. The Deep Purple days do not always do Tommy Bolin's legacy justice and this really does exemplify the necessity of giving his other work a good listen. For the same reason, both *Whips And Roses* albums are well worth a listen. *Whips And Roses I* features newly discovered takes of songs that Bolin made in the studio for the *Teaser* album. A number of instrumental jam sessions are present too. *Whips And Roses II* features alternative takes of Bolin's studio work as well as some live recordings. Both albums were released in 2006. On both *Whips And Roses* albums, it is clear that the producer, Greg Hampton, has worked hard to ensure that they deliver on sound quality. In some reviews of the *Whips And Roses* albums, fans have stated annoyance that there is no written information in the cover notes regarding personnel and where and when the recordings were made. Such is the nature of cataloguing material that, at the time, was made without anyone knowing that Bolin would not live long enough to make more great music.

Tommy Bolin's legacy lives on. In 1989, Mötley Crüe performed a cover of Tommy's song, 'Teaser'. It was for a charity compilation album called *Stairway To Heaven/Highway To Hell*. The album featured bands that performed at the Moscow Music Peace Festival. Each song is a cover of a famous solo artist or rock band who suffered a drug or alcohol-related death. The liner notes include an extensive dedication list of such artists. As was reported on 24 January 1990 in *The Washington Post*:

> Proceeds from sales will be split between the Make A Difference Foundation in North Carolina and the U.S.S.R.'s All-Union Society For Sobriety. The Make A Difference Foundation is a non-profit group directing its drug and alcohol abuse fight toward youth through pro-responsibility messages. The album project was executive produced by Bon Jovi manager Doc McGhee.

Tommy Bolin was posthumously inducted into the South Dakota Rock and Roll Music Association Hall of Fame in 2017. The official Tommy Bolin Festival has been running in Sioux City since around 1994. It celebrates his life, music and legacy. Both Tommy's brother, Johnnie, and Glenn Hughes have been proactively involved with the project over the years.

As the author of this book, I hope I have managed to tell Tommy Bolin's story in a way that does justice to his legacy. This book contains a mixture of opinions as well as a range of facts that stand up in their own right. As my telling of the Tommy Bolin story draws to a close, it matters to me that I finish with some quotes from the people who were around at the time and had the pleasure of knowing and working with Tommy in his short life. He was a talented musician who achieved a lot in such a short time. Many people who knew Tommy have a lot of very positive, kind and endearing things to say about him. It is with all the love in the world that I shall leave you with the following comments…

What a sad loss; he was on the tour when I was in 1976, and Tommy died after the first night of the tour in Miami. I heard the news the next morning. **Jeff Beck, in June 2014 in *Guitar World*.**

It was the birth of Billy Cobham laying down the f***in' backbeat, with what he knows to be the black funk and letting a cat like Bolin go crazy on top of it. It changed everybody. **Narada Michael Walden, commenting on Billy Cobham's *Spectrum* album and the impact it had on the world of fusion music in June 1999 in *Guitar Magazine*.**

As a guitar player, he was fast, yet brilliantly clean. Usually, some of these fast guys are sloppy, but his hands could move brilliantly, and each note was pure. And he showed tremendous emotion. He could cry on that guitar. **Chuck Morris, as quoted in June 1999 in *Guitar Magazine*. He booked Zephyr some gigs in some clubs in Boulder CO and went on to be an artist manager and promoter.**

When Tommy and I played together there were times when we reached incredible heights by opening up our emotions as much as we possibly could while still playing. We experienced what I can only describe as mind reading; we understood each other on a very deep level and found a way to follow the music to places we had never been before. There were a few times when we tripped on acid while we were playing and we were never the same afterwards. **David Givens, in March 2016 in *Blues Guitar*.**

I'd played with some of the best guitar players in the world, but I liked Bolin best. He could go from rock and roll to jazz to blues to funk, and he had a wonderful tone, his own distinctive sound. He didn't read music at all, but he had wonderful ears. Tommy used to play with great speed and articulation; he could play mellow, but he could also play some really, really fast riff. And unlike most rock musicians, he could play out – outside the chords for jazz improvisations. **Norma Jean Bell, in October 1989 in *Westword*.**

There were shows (where) I had tears in my eyes after, just because of the way he played.
Dave Brown, in October 1989 in *Westword*.

He had on green chiffon pantaloons, like something out of Aladdin. He was visually more exotic and flamboyant than anything I was expecting. A beautiful-looking boy. **David Coverdale, in August 2017 in *Classic Rock*.**

Tommy completely energised what was a rather distraught and headless chicken. **Jon Lord on meeting Bolin at the time of his audition for Deep Purple. Quoted posthumously in August 2017 in *Classic Rock*.**

No, I certainly wasn't ready for it (the abundance of Blackmore heckles directed at Tommy). I figured there would be some resistance, but I didn't expect to see as much as we did. What surprised me was the resistance in America. I heard many, many sustained shouts of 'Blackmore!' there, as many as I began to hear in Europe when we went there. I have to say though, on a more positive note, that Tommy very often won people over on the night. He was a considerable guitarist; let's not forget that. His abilities were astonishingly strong and when he was on a good night, he was up there with the best that I've played with. But unfortunately, those nights were few and far between. Well, maybe that's being unfair. Let's just say there weren't enough of them.
Jon Lord, as quoted posthumously in August 2017 in *Classic Rock*.

We knew Tommy was the right man for the job after the fifth or sixth bar of the first jam. He had the tone, star quality, swagger, composure, bravado… Call it arrogance, call it eccentricity, he had it in spades. He wasn't a Ritchie Blackmore clone and he had an essence, an aura about him that told us he needed to be in this band. We offered Tommy the gig on the spot.
Glenn Hughes, in August 2017 in *Classic Rock*.

Tommy was different, wasn't he? He had a very South American-flavoured, Brazilian, reggae-ish way of playing guitar; it wasn't European. It was be-boppy, it was jazz, it was everything Deep Purple weren't. He was a genius. Tommy Bolin today? I don't know if he'd have been playing an electric guitar. He would have definitely gone on further than most. Tommy would have been really avant-garde. (He) probably wouldn't have gone mainstream; Tommy would have been your Jeff Buckley of the axe. He shined brightly, and he was way ahead of his time. He was my brother and I miss him tremendously.
Glenn Hughes, in November 2016 in *Classic Rock*.

We were like brothers, so we just wrote constantly. We used to write long distance. I was in Colorado, he was living in LA. He'd call me and start playing chords over the phone. The bills were big, but so were the royalties.
Jeff Cook, in August 1987 in *Radio & Records*.

He seemed to just love music. He was into Duke Ellington and John Coltrane, Albert King to B.B. King to Hendrix – it didn't matter what style or genre it was. I about died hearing him play that ('Take Five') on guitar when he was sixteen years old. You'd hear him play songs note for note one time and then the rest of the time it would be different. I never, ever heard Tommy copy anybody.
Jeff Cook, in October 1989 in *Westword*.

Tommy was very humble about his gift, and he never made any of us feel that we weren't as good as he was. In that environment, we were able to grow, and become better players and better people.
Jeff Cook, in November 2016 in *Classic Rock*.

Tommy wanted so much to be a success not just for himself, but for the people around him, including me. He was doted on by all the big stars, I know that.
Barry Fey, in the *Tallahassee Democrat* on 8 December 1976.

He was amazing, he could have been huge. Superstars loved him, musicians loved him, the girls loved him – he just wanted to be a rock and roll star.
Barry Fey, in October 1989 in *Westword*.

He was great. He just seemed like the right guy, played the right way – a spectacular guitar player.
Dale Peters, bass player with James Gang, in November 2016 in *Classic Rock*.

All his fantastic tone was from the huge amount of power he had, as Stevie Ray Vaughn and Hendrix did.
Stanley Sheldon, bass player with Energy, in June 1999 in *Guitar Magazine*.

The good ones play what they know from the heart with great timing and understanding of what to play when. They don't play like an academic who emulates what was presented in a walled institution. They play from the experiences acquired in the real world.
Billy Cobham, in March 2018 in *The Stranger*.

Discography

Released	Recorded	Artist	Album	Context	Label
1969	1969	Zephyr	*Zephyr*	Studio	Probe
1971	1971	Zephyr	*Going Back to Colorado*	Studio	Warner Bros.
1973	1973	James Gang	*Bang*	Studio	Atco
1973	1973	Billy Cobham	*Spectrum*	Studio	Atlantic
1974	1974	James Gang	*Miami*	Studio	Atco
1975	1974	Alphonse Mouzon	*Mind Transplant*	Studio	Blue Note
1975	1975	Moxy	*Moxy*	Studio; guitar solos (6 tracks)	Polydor
1975	1975	Deep Purple	*Come Taste The Band*	Studio	Purple
1975	1975	Tommy Bolin	*Teaser*	Studio	Nemporer
2011	1975	Tommy Bolin	*Teaser Deluxe*	Remix	Nemporer
1976	1976	Tommy Bolin	Private Eyes	Studio	Columbia
1977	1975	Deep Purple	*Last Concert in Japan*	Live	Purple
2001	1975	Deep Purple	*This Time Around: Live in Tokyo*	Live Remixed & Expanded	Purple
1989	Compilation	Tommy Bolin	*The Ultimate: The Best of Tommy Bolin*	Greatest Hits	Geffen
1995 2000 2009	1976	Deep Purple	*King Biscuit Flower Hour Presents: Deep Purple in Concert / On the Wings of a Russian Foxbat*	Live	King Biscuit Flower Hour
			Deep Purple: Extended Versions Live at Long Beach 1976	Remastered	

Discography

Released	Recorded	Artist	Album	Context	Label
1996	Compilation	Tommy Bolin	*From the Archives, Vol. 1*	Outtakes	Rhino
1997	1973	Zephyr	*Zephyr Live At Art's Bar And Grill, May 2, 1973*	Live	Tommy Bolin Archives
1997	1974	Tommy Bolin & Friends	*Live at Ebbets Field 1974*	Live	Zebra
1997	1976	Tommy Bolin	*1976: In His Own Words*	Interview	Tommy Bolin Archives
1997	1976	Tommy Bolin Band	*Live at Ebbets Field 1976*	Live	Tommy Bolin Archives
1997	1976	Tommy Bolin Band	*Live at Northern Lights Recording Studio, Maynard, MA*	Live	Tommy Bolin Archives
1997	Compilation	Tommy Bolin	*The Bottom Shelf, Volume 1*	Outtakes	Tommy Bolin Archives
1997	Compilation	Tommy Bolin	*From the Archives, Volume 2*	Outtakes	Zebra
1998	1972	Energy	*The Energy Radio Broadcasts 1972*	Live	Tommy Bolin Archives
1999	1972	Energy	*Energy*	Unreleased Studio album	Tommy Bolin Archives
1999	1974	Alphonse Mouzon	*Tommy Bolin & Alphonse Mouzon Fusion Jam*	Jam Sessions	Tommy Bolin Archives
1999	Compilation	Tommy Bolin	*Come Taste the Man*	Outtakes	Tommy Bolin Archives

Discography

Released	Recorded	Artist	Album	Context	Label
1999	Compilation	Tommy Bolin	*Snapshot*	Outtakes	Purple Pyramid
2000	1975	Deep Purple	*Days May Come and Days May Go – The California Rehearsals: June 1975 and 1420 Beachwood Drive: The 1975 Rehearsals, Volume 2*	Jam Sessions	Purple
2000	1976	Tommy Bolin Band	*First Time Live*	Live	Tommy Bolin Archives
2000	Compilation	Tommy Bolin	*Naked*	Outtakes	Tommy Bolin Archives
2001	1976	Tommy Bolin Band	*Live 9/19/76*	Live	Tommy Bolin Archives
2002	1973	Billy Cobham	*Love Child: The Spectrum Sessions*	Jam Sessions	
2002	1976	Tommy Bolin Band	*Live in Miami at Jai Alai: The Final Show*	Live	Tommy Bolin Archives
2002	Compilation	Tommy Bolin	*Naked II*	Outtakes	Tommy Bolin Archives
2002	Compilation	Tommy Bolin	*After Hours: The Glen Holly Jams, Volume 1*	Jam sessions	Tommy Bolin Archives
2003	1972	Energy	*Live at Tulagi in Boulder and Rooftop Ballroom in Sioux City, December 1972*	Live	Tommy Bolin Archives

Discography

Released	Recorded	Artist	Album	Context	Label
2003	1976	Tommy Bolin Band	*Alive on Long Island*	Live	Tommy Bolin Archives
2004	Compilation	Billy Cobham	*Rudiments: The Billy Cobham Anthology*	Greatest Hits	Atlantic
2005	1976	Tommy Bolin Band	*Albany NY, September 20, 1976*	Live	Tommy Bolin Archives
2005	1976	Tommy Bolin Band	*Live at the Jet Bar*	Live	Tommy Bolin Archives
2005	1972	Energy	*Energy*	Disc 1: studio CD; Disc 2: Live at Tulagi and Rooftop Ballroom	Tommy Bolin Archives
2006	1975	Tommy Bolin	*Whips and Roses*	Teaser outtakes	Steam-hammer
2006	1975	Tommy Bolin	*Whips and Roses II*	Teaser outtakes	Steam-hammer
2008	Compilation	Tommy Bolin	*The Ultimate Redux*	Greatest Hits & outtakes	Friday Music
2011	1975-1976	Deep Purple	*Phoenix Rising*	CD: 1975/1976 tour live album; DVD: Documentary and *Rises Over Japan*	Edel
2013	Compilation	Tommy Bolin	*Whirlwind*	Outtakes	Purple Pyramid
2014	1973-1976	Tommy Bolin	*Captured Raw Jams, Vol. 1*	Jam Sessions	

Band and Album Personnel

Denny And The Triumphs

Dave Stokes: lead vocals
Brad Miller: guitar, vocals
Tommy Bolin: lead guitar (joined in 1964)
Steve Bridenbaugh: organ, vocals
Denny Foote: bass
Brad Larvick: drums

Patch Of Blue

Dave Stokes: lead vocals
Michael Schwarte: lead vocals
Tommy Bolin: lead guitar, vocals
Brad Miller: guitar, vocals
Steve Bridenbaugh: organ, vocals
George Larvick: bass, vocals
Brad Larvick: drums

The Chateaux

Bob Ellison: bass, vocals
Larry Halverson: guitar
John Bartle: guitar
Roger Rothwell: guitar
Tommy Bolin: organ and guitar
Roger Purcell: drums
Bobby Berge: drums
Mark Craney: drums

American Standard

Jeff Cook: vocals
Tommy Bolin: guitar
Terry Knieff: bass
Michael Lothamer: drums

Zephyr

Candy Givens: lead vocals, harmonica

David Givens: bass, vocals

Tommy Bolin: lead guitar, vocals

John Faris: keyboards, flute, vocals

Robbie Chamberlin: drums, vocals

Bobby Berge: drums

Zephyr was recorded at Wally Heider Studios, Los Angeles and was produced by Bill Halverson.

Going Back To Colorado was recorded at Electric Lady Studios, New York and was produced by Eddie Kramer.

Energy

Tommy Bolin: guitar

Jeff Cook: vocals, harmonica

Tom Stephenson: keyboards, vocals

Stanley Sheldon: bass

Bobby Berge: drums

Kenny Passarelli: bass

Jeremy Steig: flute

Gary Wilson: vocals

Max Gronenthal: keyboards, vocals

Russell Bizzett: drums

Archie Shelby: percussion

Billy Cobham's Spectrum album

Billy Cobham: drums, percussion

Tommy Bolin: guitar

Jan Hammer: piano, synthesiser

Lee Sklar: bass

Ron Carter: acoustic bass

Jimmy Owens: flugelhorn

Joe Farrell: flute, saxophones

Ray Barretto: congas

John Tropea: guitar (on 'Le Lis')

Spectrum was recorded at Electric Lady Studios, New York and was mixed at Trident Studios in London. It was produced by Billy Cobham.

James Gang

Roy Kenner: lead vocals, percussion

Tommy Bolin: guitar, vocals, synth

Dale Peters: bass

Jim Fox: drums, piano

Tom Dowd: keyboards, piano

Albhy Galuten: keyboards, piano

Bang was recorded at Cleveland Recording Company, Ohio. It was mixed at Atlantic Studios and was produced by all members of the band.

Miami was recorded at Criteria Recording Studios, Florida. It was mixed by all members of the band along with Tom Dowd.

Alphonse Mouzon's Mind Transplant album

Alphonse Mouzon: drums, vocals, keys

Tommy Bolin: guitar (solos on tracks: 'Snow Bound', 'Carbon Dioxide', 'Golden Rainbows', 'Nitroglycerin' and 'The Real Thing' (bonus track on later release on CD)

Jay Graydon: guitar

Lee Ritenour: guitar

Jerry Peters: keyboards

Henry Davis: bass

Rocke Grace: keyboards

Stanley Sheldon: bass

Mind Transplant was recorded at Wally Heider Studios, Los Angeles and was produced by Skip Drinkwater.

Moxy

Buzz Shearman: vocals

Earl Johnson: guitar

Buddy Caine: guitar

Terry Juric: bass:

Bill Wade: drums

Tommy Bolin: guitar (solos on tracks: 'Fantasy', 'Moon Rider', 'Time To Move On', 'Still I Wonder', 'Train' and 'Out Of Darkness')

Tom Stephenson: piano

Moxy was recorded at Sound City Studios, Los Angeles and was produced by the band and Mark Smith.

Deep Purple (Mk4)

David Coverdale: vocals

Tommy Bolin: guitar, vocals

Jon Lord: keyboards

Glenn Hughes: bass, vocals

Ian Paice: drums

Come Taste The Band was recorded at Musicland Studios, Munich. It was produced by the band and Martin Birch.

Tommy Bolin's Teaser album

Tommy Bolin: guitar, vocals

Stanley Sheldon: bass

Paul Stallworth: bass

Dave Foster: piano/synth

Jan Hammer: synth, drums

Ron Fransen: piano

Dave Sanborn: sax

Jeff Porcaro: drums

Prairie Prince: drums

Michael Walden: drums

Bobbie Berge: drums

Phil Collins: percussion

Sammy Figueroa: percussion

Rafael Cruz: percussion

Dave Brown: background vocals

Lee Kiefer: background vocals

Teaser was recorded at three different studios; The Record Plant in Los Angeles, Electric Lady Studios in New York and Trident Studios in London. It was produced by Tommy Bolin and Lee Kiefer.

The Tommy Bolin Band

(late May 1976 – late July 1976)

Tommy Bolin: guitar, vocals

Mark Stein: keyboards, vocals

Norma Jean Bell: sax, vocals

Reggie McBride: bass
Bobbie Berge: drums

(late August 1976 – early October 1976)
Tommy Bolin: guitar, vocals
Mark Stein: keyboards, vocals
Norma Jean Bell: sax, vocals
Jimmy Haslip: bass
Johnnie Bolin: drums

(early October 1976 – December 3, 1976)
Tommy Bolin: guitar, vocals
Max Gronenthal: keyboards, vocals
Norma Jean Bell: sax,vocals
Jimmy Haslip: bass
Mark Craney: drums

Tommy Bolin's Private Eyes album

Tommy Bolin: guitar, piano, vocals
Mark Stein: keyboards, vocals
Norma Jean Bell: sax, percussion, vocals
Reggie McBride: bass, vocals
Bobby Berge: drums, percussion
Bobbye Hall: percussion
Carmine Appice: drums on 'Someday Will Bring Our Love Home'
Del Newman: string arrangements on 'Hello, Again'

Private Eyes was recorded at both Cherokee Studios, Los Angeles and Trident Studios, London. It was produced by Tommy Bolin and Dennis MacKay.

Tommy Bolin's Live Performances

This list features the dates of known live performances. I sourced the information from released recordings, vintage concert reviews, fan sites (both related to Bolin and some of the other mentioned acts). Where possible, I made sure to check that the information corroborated with ticket stubs and posters. It is very likely that this list is not complete.

American Standard

(All performed at The Family Dog in Denver CO)

1967

October 21: American Standard plus other local bands

December 21: A Benefit for Sharie Duncan (an injured student) featuring Allman Joy, Eighth Penny Matter, Leopold Fuchs, Jimmerfield Legend and American Standard

1968

January 12 & 13: Beggars Opera Company, American Standard, Eighth Penny Matter

February 9 & 10: American Standard and Leopold Fuchs H. Bomb

February 14: American Standard and guest appearance by Jimi Hendrix

Zephyr

1969

Feb 28, March 1-2: Avalon Ballroom San Francisco CA with Love and Mad River

March 28-29: Aquarius Theater Phoenix AZ with Jethro Tull

April 10-13: Fillmore West San Francisco CA with Jeff Beck Group, and Aynsley Dunbar

May 26-29: Boston Tea Party Boston MA with Led Zeppelin

June 28 & 29: Mile High Stadium Denver CO Denver Pop Festival

July 3: Reed's Ranch Colorado Springs CO with Grateful Dead

July 27: State Fair Park Milwaukee WI Mid West Rock Festival

August 16: Earl Warren Showgrounds Santa Barbara CA Blind Faith Festival

November 29: Denver Coliseum Denver CO with Crosby, Stills, Nash & Young and Santana

December 12: McFarlin Auditorium Dallas TX with Grateful Dead

1970

January 2-3: Eagles Auditorium Seattle WA with Spirit and Bread

January 22-25: Fillmore West San Francisco CA Albert King with Lee Michaels as scheduled but replaced Savoy Brown

February 6: The Warehouse New Orleans LA with Jack Bruce and White Clover

February 17: Nicholson Pavilion Ellensburg WA with John Mayall and Duster Bennett

February 20: Seattle Center Arena Seattle WA with John Mayall and Duster Bennett

February 26: Fillmore East New York NY with Ten Years After and John Hammond

February 27-28: Fillmore East New York NY with Ten Years After and Doug Kershaw

March 8: Magoo's New City Opera House Minneapolis MN with Spirit

March 26-28: Boston Tea Party Boston MA with Lee Michaels and Rod Stewart & Faces

April 10-11: Ludlow Garage Cincinnati OH with Argent

April 15: Federal Building Denver CO with Jane Fonda's Anti-War Protest

April 16: Hemis Fair Arena San Antonio TX with Joe Cocker and Leon Russell

April 17-18: Mammoth Gardens Denver CO with Jethro Tull and Clouds

April 23: Glenn Miller Ballroom Boulder CO with Judy Roderick

May 17: Swing Auditorium San Bernardino CA with Joe Cocker, Geronimo Black, and Grin

June 13: Crosley Field Cincinnati OH Cincinnati Summer Pop Festival

July 19: Almeda Speedway Houston TX Day of Joy Festival

August 8-9: Turner Falls Park Davis OK Turner Falls International Pop Festival

August 11: Civic Auditorium Santa Monica CA with Mountain and Wolfgang

August 14: Mammoth Gardens Denver CO

August 22: Wollman Rink New York NY Schaefer Festival

1971

February 5: Colorado State University Fort Collins CO

April 30: Portland Sports Arena Portland OR with Blues Image

May 1: Salem Armory Salem OR with Blues Image

May 4: Cromwell Field Los Angeles CA with Sweetwater and Ballin' Jack

March 5: Civic Auditorium Santa Monica CA with Mountain

Deep Purple
November 1975

8: International Center Arena Honolulu, Hawaii, USA

13: Western Springs Stadium Auckland, New Zealand

17: Queen Elizabeth II Park Christchurch, New Zealand

19: Hordern Pavilion Sydney, Australia

20: Hordern Pavilion Sydney, Australia

21: Hordern Pavilion Sydney, Australia

22: Brisbane Milton Tennis Courts Brisbane, Australia

25: Festival Hall Melbourne, Australia

26: Festival Hall Melbourne, Australia

27: Memorial Drive Adelaide, Australia

December 1975

1: Perth WACA Perth, Australia

4: Senayan Main Stadium Jakarta, Indonesia

5: Senayan Main Stadium Jakarta, Indonesia

8: Shi Kokaido (City Hall) Nagoya, Japan

11: Kosei Nenkin Hall Osaka, Japan

12: Kyuden Kinen Taiikulan Fukuoka, Japan

15: Budokan Tokyo, Japan

January 1976

14: Fort Bragg Fayetteville, North Carolina, USA

15: The Capital Centre Landover, Maryland, USA

18: The Spectrum Philadelphia, Pennsylvania, USA

19: Providence Civic Centre Providence, Rhode Island, USA

22: Radio City Music Hall New York, USA

23: Radio City Music Hall New York, USA

24: Boston Music Hall Boston, Massachusetts, USA

26: Springfield Civic Centre Springfield, Massachusetts, USA

27: Hersheypark Arena Hershey, Pennsylvania, USA

28: War Memorial Rochester, New York, USA

30: Greensboro Coliseum Greensboro, North Carolina, USA

31: Freedom Hall Johnson City, Tennessee, USA

February 1976

1: St. John's Arena Columbus, Ohio, USA

3: Omni Atlanta, Georgia, USA

4: Municipal Auditorium Birmingham, Alabama, USA

6: Civic Centre Lakeland, Florida, USA

8: Jai Alai Fronton Miami, Florida, USA

11: Horton Field House Bloomington-Normal, Illinois, USA

12: Cobo Arena Detroit, Michigan, USA

13: Hara Arena Dayton, Ohio, USA

15: Dane County Memorial Coliseum Madison, Wisconsin, USA

17: Fairgrounds Arena Oklahoma City, Oklahoma, USA

18: Convention Centre Arena San Antonio, Texas, USA

19: Taylor County Auditorium Abilene, Texas, USA

21: Tarrant County Convention Centre Forth Worth, Texas, USA

22: Sam Houston Coliseum Houston, Texas, USA

24: County Coliseum El Paso, Texas, USA

27: Long Beach Arena Los Angeles, California, USA

28: Swing Auditorium San Bernadino, California, USA

29: Tempe Stadium Tempe, Arizona, USA

March 1976

2: Salt Palace Salt Lake City, Utah, USA

4: Denver Auditorium Arena Denver, Colorado, USA

11: Granby Hall Leicester, UK

12: Empire Pool Wembley, London, UK

13: Empire Pool Wembley, London, UK

14: The Apollo Glasgow, UK

15: Empire Theatre Liverpool, UK

Tommy Bolin Band
April 1976

28: La Paloma Theatre, Encinitas CA

30: The Roxy Theatre, W. Hollywood CA

May 1976

1: The Roxy Theatre W,. Hollywood CA

2: Tempe Stadium, Tempe AZ with Robin Trower and REO Speedwagon

6: Winterland, San Francisco CA with Robin Trower, Heart and Steve Marriott

13: Ebbets Fields, Denver CO

22: My Fathers Place, Roslyn NY

24-26: The Bottom Line, New York NY

July 1976

13: Convention Centre Arena, San Antonio TX with Moxy

18: Electric Ballroom, Dallas TX

20: Armadillo World Headquarters, Austin TX

August 1976

29: Mile High Stadium, Denver CO

September 1976

19 & 20: Palace Theatre Albany NY with Blue Öyster Cult

21: Shaboo Inn, Willimantic CT

22: Northern Recording Studio, Maynard, MA

24: Aragon Ballroom, Chicago IL

29 & 30: My Fathers Place, Roslyn NY

October 1976

2: Tower Theatre, Philadelphia PA

3: Tomorrow, Youngstown OH

4: Cleveland Agora, Cleveland OH

5: Ford Theatre, Detroit MI

8: Rev's Flying Circus, Waukesha WI

24: Santa Monica Civic Auditorium, Santa Monica CA

25 & 26: Paramount Theatre, Seattle WA

28: Paramount Theatre, Seattle WA with Rush

29: National Guard Armory, Tacoma WA with Rush

30: Paramount Theatre, Portland Oregon with Rush

31: Convention Centre Spokane, Washington with Rush

November 1976

3: Douglas Hall Fairgrounds, Roseburg OR with Rush

4: Medford Armory, Medford OR with Rush

5 & 6: Winterland, San Francisco CA with The Elvin Bishop Group

7: Sacramento Memorial Auditorium, Sacramento CA

10: Tulsa Fairgrounds Pavilion, Tulsa OK

11: McNichols Sports Arena, Denver CO

13: Electric Ballroom, Dallas TX

16: Jazz City Studios, New Orleans LA

19: RKO Orpheum Theatre, Davenport IA with Pure Prairie League

21: Bradley Fieldhouse, Peoria IL

22: Municipal Auditorium, Sioux City IA

December 1976

3: Jai Alai Fronton, Miami FL with Jeff Beck

On Track series

Queen – Andrew Wild 978-1-78952-003-3
Emerson Lake and Palmer – Mike Goode 978-1-78952-000-2
Deep Purple and Rainbow 1968-79 – Steve Pilkington 978-1-78952-002-6
Yes – Stephen Lambe 978-1-78952-001-9
Blue Oyster Cult – Jacob Holm-Lupo 978-1-78952-007-1
The Beatles – Andrew Wild 978-1-78952-009-5
Roy Wood and the Move – James R Turner 978-1-78952-008-8
Genesis – Stuart MacFarlane 978-1-78952-005-7
Jethro Tull – Jordan Blum 978-1-78952-016-3
The Rolling Stones 1963-80 – Steve Pilkington 978-1-78952-017-0
Judas Priest – John Tucker 978-1-78952-018-7
Toto – Jacob Holm-Lupo 978-1-78952-019-4
Van Der Graaf Generator – Dan Coffey 978-1-78952-031-6
Frank Zappa 1966 to 1979 – Eric Benac 978-1-78952-033-0
Elton John in the 1970s – Peter Kearns 978-1-78952-034-7
The Moody Blues – Geoffrey Feakes 978-1-78952-042-2
The Beatles Solo 1969-1980 – Andrew Wild 978-1-78952-030-9
Steely Dan – Jez Rowden 978-1-78952-043-9
Hawkwind – Duncan Harris 978-1-78952-052-1
Fairport Convention – Kevan Furbank 978-1-78952-051-4
Iron Maiden – Steve Pilkington 978-1-78952-061-3
Dream Theater – Jordan Blum 978-1-78952-050-7
10CC and Godley and Crème – Peter Kearns 978-1-78952-054-5
Gentle Giant – Gary Steel 978-1-78952-058-3
Kansas – Kevin Cummings 978-1-78952-057-6
Mike Oldfield – Ryan Yard 978-1-78952-060-6
The Who – Geoffrey Feakes 978-1-78952-076-7
Crosby, Stills and Nash – Andrew Wild 978-1-78952-039-2
U2 – Eoghan Lyng 978-1-78952-078-1
Barclay James Harvest – Keith and Monika Domone 978-1-78952-067-5
Steve Hackett – Geoffrey Feakes 978-1-78952-098-9
Renaissance – David Detmer 978-1-78952-062-0
Dire Straits – Andrew Wild 978-1-78952-044-6
Camel – Hamish Kuzminski 978-1-78952-040-8
Rush – Will Romano 978-1-78952-080-4
Joni Mitchell – Peter Kearns 978-1-78952-081-1
UFO – Richard James 978-1-78952-073-6
Kate Bush – Bill Thomas 978-1-78952-097-2
Asia – Pete Braidis 978-1-78952-099-6
Aimee Mann – Jez Rowden 978-1-78952-036-1
Pink Floyd Solo – Mike Goode 978-1-78952-046-0
Gong – Kevan Furbank 978-1-78952-082-8

Decades Series
Pink Floyd in the 1970s – Georg Purvis 978-1-78952-072-9
Marillion in the 1980s – Nathaniel Webb 978-1-78952-065-1
Focus in the 1970s – Stephen Lambe 978-1-78952-079-8
Curved Air in the 1970s – Laura Shenton 978-1-78952-069-9

On Screen series
Carry On... – Stephen Lambe 978-1-78952-004-0
Seinfeld Seasons 1 to 5 – Stephen Lambe 978-1-78952-012-5
Monty Python – Steve Pilkington 978-1-78952-047-7
Doctor Who: The David Tennant Years – Jamie Hailstone 978-1-78952-066-8
James Bond – Andrew Wild 978-1-78952-010-1
David Cronenberg – Patrick Chapman 978-1-78952- 071-2

Other Books
Maximum Darkness – Deke Leonard 978-1-78952-048-4
The Twang Dynasty – Deke Leonard 978-1-78952-049-1
Tommy Bolin: In and Out of Deep Purple – Laura Shenton 978-1-78952-070-5
Jon Anderson and the Warriors - the road to Yes – David Watkinson 978-1-78952-059-0
Derek Taylor: For Your Radioactive Children - Andrew Darlington 978-1-78952-038-5
20 Walks Around Tewkesbury – Stephen Lambe 978-1-78952-074-3

and many more to come!

Would you like to write for Sonicbond Publishing?

At Sonicbond Publishing we are always on the look-out for authors, particularly for our two main series:

On Track. Mixing fact with in depth analysis, the On Track series examines the work of a particular musical artist or group. All genres are considered from easy listening and jazz to 60s soul to 90s pop, via rock and metal.

On Screen. This series looks at the world of film and television. Subjects considered include directors, actors and writers, as well as entire television and film series. As with the On Track series, we balance fact with analysis.

While professional writing experience would, of course, be an advantage the most important qualification is to have real enthusiasm and knowledge of your subject. First-time authors are welcomed, but the ability to write well in English is essential.

Sonicbond Publishing has distribution throughout Europe and North America, and all books are also published in E-book form. Authors will be paid a royalty based on sales of their book.

Further details are available from www.sonicbondpublishing.co.uk. To contact us, complete the contact form there or email info@sonicbondpublishing.co.uk